Eat Local

Simple Steps to Enjoy Real, Healthy & Affordable Food

T0116751

New World Publishing
Auburn, California

Eat Local
Simple Steps to Enjoy Real, Healthy & Affordable Food

By Jasia Steinmetz

Publisher's Cataloging-in-Publication
(Provided by Quality Books, Inc.)

Steinmetz, Jasia.
   Eat local : simple steps to enjoy real,
healthy & affordable food / Jasia Steinmetz ; cover
painting by Jan Kapple Klein.
      p. cm.
      Includes index.
      ISBN-13: 978-0-9632814-5-6
      ISBN-10: 0-9632814-5-3

   1. Food supply--United States. 2. Local foods.
   3. Community-supported agriculture. 4. Farmers' markets.
   5. Grocery shopping.   I. Title.

HD9005.S74 2011   641.3'1
                     QBI11-600050

New World Publishing
11543 Quartz Dr. #1
Auburn, CA 95602
www.nwpub.net

Dedication

This book is dedicated to all the farmers who feed us, care for the land and maintain our rural communities in one of the oldest and most noble professions, and to my family, especially Jeff, my husband, who support me in all my dreams and endeavors.

Table of Contents

Introduction

Chapter 1: Introduction

Eating food is simple act: Consume food that is available near you. Yet it also a profound act since we choose food based on our family influences, the environment, politics, etc. In fact, each time you raise your fork or cup to your lips, you are voting.

Like many, with the increasing food products introduced in stores and restaurants, more was better and I hardly thought about voting with my food choices. Yet as a clinical dietitian, I saw the effects of food choices and abundance as I counseled healthier food choices daily to my patients. Now, as a community nutritionist, I think about food in different ways, identifying with the hungry and finding root causes for the lack of affordable, nourishing food. I have learned about the strong ties of food to culture and the different ethnic grocery stores that can transport me to a different place.

In frequent conversations with farmers, I am startled to find that many qualify for food stamps or need off-farm jobs to keep the farm and afford health insurance. I learn about the loss of topsoil, the cost of agricultural inputs and the challenges of cheap food. I now know root cellaring foods, best salsa tomatoes and asparagus foraging. As I connect with farmers and community, I connect with food.

Food choices are journeys. My parents grew up with a small urban garden, which did not explain my father's limited tolerance for only five or six vegetables. Their post-depression memories combined with post-war technologies shaped our frugal yet modern household foods – inexpensive canned vegetables and Tang® orange drink powder – the drink of the astronauts. I loved the latest techno-food: White bread, Velveeta® cheese (technically, cheese food) and Spam®. I distinctly remember "making" breakfast as young child, excitedly climbing up on the kitchen counter in the morning as my parents slept and heating the latest invention, pastries that were shaped to fit into the toaster.

In the city, local food was everything in the neighborhood grocery store. After my family moved to a small rural town, I discovered the details of milking cows and realized the nearby hill named "sugar bush" referred to all the maple trees tapped for syrup. During my youth, local food was everything in the neighborhood grocery store. Nature and food started to connect.

"Local" is in the news frequently and for many reasons: We are encouraged to find local food, feed it to our families and support it in our communities. This call is not limited to our personal lives; it can be heard in our schools, hospitals, restaurants. A few decades have eroded our knowledge of where our food is grown and where we obtain food. If we do not have gardens, how do we know when to start plants, what grows above or below ground, or when to harvest? How can we anticipate which foods will be available at a farmers' market? What are the seasons of food? What variety of peach makes the best pie?

As a city dweller, I thought of seasons strictly as climate, marked in the Midwest by winter snow, spring rain, mildly hot summers, breezy cooling, then a return to snow. If I had to think about seasonality in food, it was as broad changes in the produce section in the grocery store. Since apples, oranges and bananas were always available in the supermarket, I never considered these to have a season. Peaches, cherries, watermelon, corn-on-the-cob and "leaf" lettuce were occasional and, therefore, seasonal foods. I rarely connected food with a place where it grew. Even more remote was the notion of "terrier," connecting a specific food to the particular soil and weather that imparts specific flavors to the food. I knew that my tomatoes from the garden tasted better than the store's; carrots were sweeter after a slight frost and strawberries could be picked by the crate. As the garden and orchard got bigger with kids, my cooking and preservation skills grew and my tastes changed. Farm food became less daunting; my friends taught me specialties from their countries using their native varieties of vegetables, and restaurants featured local farmers' products.

As a college professor, I focus on food every day, whether discussing in the classroom, cooking in the kitchen lab or giving workshops. I help others see the connection between their meal and the rest – people, land and politics. I talk with farmers, chefs, truckers, children – everyone and anyone who eats. Mostly, I learn about the impact of voting with our forks, and changing a system with each bite.

The seasons are food related. The first greens of spring, the strawberries of early summer, abundance of summer crops and the dense root crops – carrots, parsnips, potatoes, etc. I wrote this book to help and hasten your journey to local food. Our increasing remoteness from food and farming, the growing obesity at young ages and the loss of small farms reflect a runaway food system. This book helps you bring it back home. I hope you and your family celebrate food and its source, no matter where you live.

We determine the food system. By our daily purchases, we vote for the food that is available. Our food system is constantly changing and we determine this change with our purchases. This book alerts you to the innovation happening in communities across our nation. I also alert you to the current food system that feeds many people but is now threatening the very foundations of our lives.

How can we control our food supply now and for the future? A successful food system depends on the innovation of farmers. Food producers and distributors in your community assure that healthy food is available near you. Fresh and minimally processed food purchased close to harvest is the real food that we value.

Tuck the book in your pocket or purse for a ready source of information as you discover local food. In each section, I give you a brief introduction to a place or person that helps you find local food, such as a farmer, grocer, or market. This is followed by the first steps to get you started – questions to ask a farmer, where to find real food, signs and labels to look for, etc. I want you to feel comfortable talking to the people that provide your food. In addition, if you decide that you want to grow some of your own food, I will point you to sources for that, too. Lastly, I give you more suggestions for taking control of our food system so that our children and future generations will have healthy, real food.

The great news is that there are many people who are eager to help you find the delectable food that is grown near you. So start where you are most interested... and good eating!

Chapter 2:
Our Runaway Food System
(Why We Need Local)

I was in early grade school when my parents owned Kit's Kozy Korner, a mom and pop burger joint. I loved the business of the counter service and the coziness of the booths, thinking this was the hip place to be. I thought, "This is what I will be when I grow up, a waitress here. I will start with the soda machine; move to the soft serve ice cream and then, waitress when I am a big girl." At first, I felt that I had hit the kid's jackpot: We lived above the restaurant with the hamburgers, French fries and soda, which I translated as easy, daily access. All my friends ate homemade food but my parents spent their hours behind the counter making burgers, fries and other foods that could be easily transformed in a deep-fat fryer and small grill. Surely, I dreamed our diet would include these often.

Disappointingly, my parents considered fast food as treats, and allowed it only for childhood birthday parties or occasional sleepovers. My parents insisted that we have a home cooked meal as a family upstairs at the kitchen table each night rather than eat our inventory downstairs. Instead of being the special child who could have frequent access to fast food, I was at the family table upstairs, eating liver, potatoes, vegetables and fruit like all my friends. Our kitchen had the basic ingredients that supported the good meals my parents wanted for their children.

When I left home, my diet – like everyone else's – shifted away from simple, healthy meals to highly processed foods. Alarming shifts in our food choices have occurred in the last three decades as we frequently and increasingly eat processed foods. These are not the minimally processed, canned veg-
etables or frozen fruits, but rather highly processed products such as fast foods, bakery, and sugar-sweetened beverages which lose vital nutrients and take on fats and sugars. The resulting consequence is increased obesity in children that compromises their adulthood. One-third of the children born in 2000 are expected to develop diabetes in their lifetime. The food that we expect to nourish our children and guarantee health is being undermined by our runaway food system.

The food industry has grown enormously: industrial farming has thousands of acres of crops or animals; food is traded on the stock market as commodities; and grocery stores have become mega-stores. We expect our food system to provide the food necessary to feed us as our population changes and to be productive for children and grandchildren, yet there are clear indications that our current system is jeopardizing the ability of future generations while we are compromising the very foundation that we depend on. Decisions are being made now about our food production that will affect the food system far into the future.

Experts are concerned about this runaway food system that has become very powerful and uncontrolled.[1] This runaway system is threatening the very systems vital to our well-being, almost by accident. Agricultural pollution is the leading impact on our rivers and lakes. Pesticides and herbicides used on our food are permanently altering our soil and water with unknown health risks to growers and consumers. We are eating the genetically engineered food that is changing the nature of plants and animals. Before we have time to understand the ocean as one enormous ecosystem, the huge fishing nets that drag the ocean floor are altering life and contributing to declining fish stocks.

The good news is that Americans are finding ways to control this runaway food system before it does more damage to the foundations of our health and well-being. By "voting with our forks," we are taking thoughtful actions to determine the direction of our food system. Supporting food and food policies that sustain the foundations of good eating and supporting agriculture is an investment in our future. The local food movement is contributing in significant ways, encouraging individual choices that support everyone from farmers to healthy families while safeguarding the environment.

In our current system, food typically travels thousands of miles, often across international borders. By forcing our farmers to compete on a global market, our agricultural economies are undermined and farmers forced out. Rather than lose the knowledge and ability of our local agriculture and compromise our ability to feed ourselves in the future, many communities are finding ways to support a local food system. Purchasing food directly from your local farmer helps your farmer earn more of your food dollars which otherwise would go to packaging, processing and marketing; your farmer invests more in the community, and you take home fresh, nutrition-rich food.

1 Bales, Susan Nall (2006). Framing the Food System. Washington, DC: Frame-Works Institute.

Many communities have taken innovative steps by promoting locally produced foods in grocery stores and schools and increasing farmers' markets. Choosing these foods supports the local economy and safeguards the future of farming while providing food that tastes great.

Food and our environment are inextricably bound together. The geography, climate and natural resources in an area determine its food production capability, and diets have evolved over time to satisfy cultural and health needs. Yet in recent times, with the addition of advertising-induced artificial tastes and "needs," food production has become increasingly expensive for the environment. We must consider the environmental capabilities and impact of our current food system that supports short-term decisions with long-term consequences. We can make food choices that support our local communities and land as well as other countries' resources. We must source our food in the most conscientious way possible while maintaining resources for future generations and still providing adequate food. Local foods, sustainably produced, are a key component to the ideal, healthy diet.

We need to encourage a food system that makes whole foods available for everyone – this is especially important for families with children. Healthy eating is neither complicated nor time consuming – fruits and vegetables can be eaten raw; dairy is sold ready to eat. Family meals at home require a few basic cooking skills, but nothing fancy. Most foods need only simple cooking such as boiling, pan frying, baking or microwaving.

What will it take to increase wholesome, fresh foods and decrease our reliance on fast food, and processed food? It is up to us as a society to determine what our food system looks like. We can make small daily changes to maintain our health now and support a food system that will provide for our future needs. Eating local is an enjoyable first step.

Eating for our best health is not a complicated formula. Wise parents and grandparents hand down the basic foundation of good eating in every generation in every country. This universal but simple knowledge includes the following "simple steps."

Simple Steps to Good Eating!

🍎 Eat food grown by people you know.

🍎 Eat without compromising nature.

🍎 Eat different foods during the day, every day.

🍎 Eat when we are hungry and stop when we are nearly full.

🍎 Eat with gratitude amongst family and friends in a pleasing environment.

🍎 Eat simply with whole foods that require little cooking or processing.

🍎 Find food grown in your area.

Chapter 3: Why Eat Local Food?

Each spring, a local farmer starts my tomato plants from a variety of seeds he has saved over the years. The exotic names – *Tolbasc, Rasta, Paul Robeson, Soldacki* – and the descriptions – *ruby, pink, deep purple, green striped, long, meaty, sweet, tart, or zingy* – make me wish the harvest was here. To describe a tomato as a generic red bulb would be impossible, now that local tomatoes are a part of my life.

Food has value beyond consumption, and local food directly reflects the values of our region, our heritage, our culture and our communities. Local food is a celebration of what the land offers both through the hands of the farmers who bring it to our local markets and through the bounty of our home gardens served at our family tables. We celebrate the flow of food from land to table in our festivals and holidays.

Food is amongst our strongest memories: the sight and smell of food are strong triggers for remembering family meals, weddings, favorite birthdays and other passages of life. For many immigrants, food is the umbilical cord to the culture left behind and connections to their new country. Since our bodies are built from the food we eat, our food history literally is part of who we are and where we come from. Every cell in our body and in the bodies of all our relatives before us reflects the DNA of the foods our families have eaten for generations.

Local food captures the place where it was grown. The unique characteristics of the food originate in the distinctiveness of the soil that nourished it; the topography of the land, whose altitude and exposure help to shape microclimates in fields and woods throughout the growing season; and the overall climate of the region. In  spring, when cows and goats are back in the pasture and new plants are in the field, we can taste this in the cheese. That is because the milk includes the color and compounds from new grasses of the local fields-clover, rye, dandelions, and early grasses help to make spring cheddar different from fall cheddar.

Celebrate culture, community & connection. Food comes from the hands and hearts of our relatives and friends, passing on their culinary secrets and helping to maintain our cultural connections – how to grow beans that have been in your family for generations, make pickles like your grandmother, or roll the chapati in a perfect circle taught by a friend. Each culture celebrates with its own distinctive food and food customs, and many communities celebrate these with local festivals: Stevens Point Wisconsin's Spud Bowl, Gilroy California's Garlic Festival and Poteet Texas' Strawberry Festival. Our community, like New Orleans, celebrates the start of Lent with our own version of Mardi Gras, but with polkas and jelly doughnuts called paczki. Maintaining our cultural and community connections is an important role of food in our lives, connecting us to our neighbors, ancestors and religion.

Celebrate your local agriculture. Every plot and region of land on earth is unique with different growing conditions, and food that is grown locally reflects the skills and knowledge of the people who farm or garden the land. Through years of working a plot of land, local growers develop an intimacy with their land as they observe interrelations of plants, insects and animals  through all seasons and conditions. This supplies an encyclopedia of agriculture and eating local food celebrates this heritage. Buying from local farmers ensures the legacy of farming in your area and supports agriculture as a vital occupation within your community.

Celebrate variety and biodiversity. You may have noticed that chain grocers distribute similar food on a national level. Many grocers stock Cortland, MacIntosh, and Delicious apples – all common types that remain from the 14,000 named varieties we formerly had in the U.S. The 1905 seed catalogs and other literature identified 6,554 apple varieties. Currently, only 3,000 varieties are accessible to the public, and many heritage apple varieties, with names like Black Twig (Alabama), Spitzenburg (New Hampshire), Grimes Gold (Colorado), and Wolf River (Wisconsin), are only available locally. Maintaining a healthy variety of plants is our insurance against pests and diseases of the future and fosters biodiversity within an area. Our local seeds have family histories, as immigrants often carried their seeds to their new home, crossing their plants with native plants to create new varieties.

Celebrate the seasons! The world over celebrates the seasons with the coming and going of food. Spring peas, watermelon in summer, and pumpkins in fall – each food has its time. Local food celebrates the seasons where you live. Spring in our area finds people searching the woods, streams, and ditches, foraging for ramps, asparagus, morels and watercress. Summer raspberries are abundant in fields and roadsides. Only recently, I learned how my older relatives of Polish and Russian heritage were known for their mushroom knowledge and foraging skills throughout the growing seasons.

Celebrate local tastes. Local food is food that is so distractingly delicious, you stop what you are doing just to taste, smell and look at the food. Food that is so luscious, you want to say to someone, "You've just got to taste this!" urging your children, friends and neighbors to experience it. Remember the green of fresh spinach or the robust red of the tomato, the juicy look of strawberries, and the rich creaminess of cheese? A fresh pear or apple has an aroma of the sun and trees and flowers, both earthy and perfumed. Then there is the distinctive feel on your tongue, smooth or pebbly, each bite a celebration of the season. You want to remember the experience of eating the food and to share the experience.

Celebrate health. Local, fresh food contains more nutrients because we purchase within a day or two after harvest so it can stay on the vine or in the field longer than food transported long distances. Nutritional value declines, often dramatically, as time passes after harvest, and the short time from field to market for local food reduces nutrient loss. Without prepackaging, you can also buy in smaller quantities with more variety, which can result in better health. Another benefit of local food is your ability to ask the farmer about production practices, especially chemicals used during production, and other food safety questions.

Celebrate farmers and farmland. Support-ing your area farmers assures a food supply into the future and helps build a stronger community. Talking with farmers alerts you to the challenges of growing food, the abundance in each season, and the issues that affect the food supply surrounding your community. By supporting farmers  who use sustainable practices, you preserve the environment for generations. Local farmers are the best teachers for learning about your food and often share recipes and preservation tips.

Celebrate saving your money and increas-ing community money. Buying directly from the farmer saves you money. Of-ten prices in the farmers' market are comparable to or less than those at a grocery store because there are fewer re-  sources involved in getting the food to you. Freshly harvested food lasts longer, saving you more money. In the conventional food system, a farmer receives less than twenty cents for every food dollar you spend, the rest spent on marketing, process-ing and distributing. In addition, most of your money spent at the chain store leaves your community. Buying from a locally owned store, on the other hand, doubles or triples the amount you spend for local use, as your dollars circulate to other local businesses like the seed company or farm implement dealer.

The remaining chapters of this book explain these benefits in detail and give you the information you need to incorporate more local food in your meals.

Top Reasons for Buying Local

🍎 Celebrate your family food heritage.

🍎 Perk up all your senses with fresh food.

🍎 Honor local farmers and their knowledge.

🍎 Preserve nature and farmland for future generations.

🍎 Save money while investing in your community.

🍎 Improve your health.

🍎 Maintain the biodiversity of species.

🍎 Know your food; ask questions about food safety.

Chapter 4: Concerns & Challenges

You may agree with some or all of the reasons for local eating, but still have many questions. Let's talk about the most common concerns and challenges of eating local.

I have a membership to a large discount store. How is eating local less expensive?

Eating local supports your efforts to save money. Memberships in both discount stores and buying cooperatives can save money and stretch your food dollars. Shop for value first; the best value is the food that is the most nutrient rich for the dollar. Design your menu around health and taste first; then fit other foods into your budget. Buying staples at either type of store may be a worthwhile investment while getting produce or dairy locally.

My friend told me that local food costs more. How can I stay within my food budget?

Three simple steps will help you eat well and affordably. First, develop and follow a food budget. Know where your food dollars are going and why you purchase specific foods routinely. Secondly, gradually incorporate local food into your routine. Local food smells and tastes great but loses its appeal in the back of your fridge after a few weeks. You are building a life of healthy eating – have fun with small, meaningful changes. Third, choose the local food that is most important to you. Eating has value when it supports who we are. Which one of these is a priority: health, convenience, community, environment, spirituality?

I like the convenience of doing all my shopping at one store – am I spending more gas money just to buy local?

The proximity and convenience of local foods may surprise you, as local food is often available within your favorite grocery store, in a farmers' market in the grocer's parking lot, or in community space nearby. You can also plan your shopping route to access local food in various markets. A Community Supported Agriculture (CSA) farmer may deliver to your work or near your home. Save gas by carpooling, biking, walking or taking the bus no matter where you shop.

I love eating out each week. Do I have to stay home and cook to eat local?

Many chefs are rediscovering the vibrant tastes of local food. Restaurant owners respond to consumer demand and are likely to respond to your request to put local on the menu. Ask the owner or chef for items that include local ingredients or notice menu items or specials with the farm names near special foods, such as Barnard Orchard plums.

I enjoy convenience foods. Will I have to take a cooking class to eat local?

Many local foods such as fruit, vegetables and cheese are grab-and-go foods. You can incorporate local foods as snacks or start with a few substitutions for your current convenience foods. Many farmers' markets sell bakery items and canned products such as jams, jellies, salsa or other sauces.

I did not recognize many of the foods at the farmers' market and did not want to spend money on food I may not enjoy. How can I eat local when I don't have money to waste on food I won't like?

Farmer's markets change with the season, and you may have visited at a time when there were new foods for you. If you can't find your favorite foods, ask the farmer when it will be at the market or obtain a list of seasonal foods from your area. Have a tasting party with new foods, where each friend brings a food unfamiliar to them.

My kids are picky eaters. How can we eat local as a family?

It takes between 15 - 20 exposures to a new food before children and adults ultimately decide to reject or accept foods. Children are known for their food jags so don't get discouraged and continue to expose your children to new foods.

I live in the northern states where we have 3 - 4 months of winter. Do I have to eat preserved food all the time if I want to eat local?

Northern climates often stock locally sourced food, such as dairy products, in grocery stores. Winter farmers' markets are increasing, with storage crops such as onions, potatoes, squash, garlic and apples available. Local food that is preserved (such as sauces, jellies, and jams), as well as brined foods (such as sauerkraut and pickles), are also available. You can continue to include local food in your diet all year round in every state.

Our farmers' market is small and it looks like the sellers are getting the produce from a warehouse or distributor and reselling it. How can I be sure that the farmers are selling local food?

Growing conditions can change within a state so that certain crops may be available 2 - 3 weeks earlier just south of you. There may also be favorable conditions just across your state border. Ask the seller where the food was grown and be sure to get the name of the farm or location. The definition of local can vary from market to market. We define local in our market as grown within the state, rather than county. Some farmers' markets have rules that restrict sales exclusively for local food but you need to check their definition of local. There are more tips in the farmers' markets chapter.

What about the headlines about contaminants and/ or dangerous pathogens found in non-processed, local foods?

Food safety is an important issue since food pathogens can adapt much faster than human technology. Pathogens may exist in many parts of our food system, whether food is processed or non-processed. The safety of the food supply is dependent on accountability and inspection. Tracing food production keeps the producer accountable and is possible with a localized food system rather than a nationally distributed system. The recent spinach contamination was possible on such a wide scale in many states precisely because it was produced in large quantities and shipped through many channels. The USDA and FDA do not have enough staff to inspect every shipment of food that enters the country or is produced and transported. Food that goes through multiple handlers also has more opportunities for contamination. Local food may be safer for several reasons: fewer people handle the food; the farmer's reputation is directly dependent on his customer's health; and the food is usually sold as a whole so there is less entry for contaminants. See Part II for suggested questions to ask your farmer so you feel confident about the food you are eating.

I really like my supermarket variety. Aren't local foods limited?

Local foods typically in farmers' markets or farm stands offer more variety than the grocery stores, where there is usually very little seasonal variety. Many foods found in your area are too delicate to ship or are grown in supplies too small for grocery store demand but provide a niche market for smaller farmers. Farmers also grow different varieties of the same produce. For instance, our local farmer grows 20 different types of potatoes, each with a slightly different flavor. Local farmers may also use heritage seeds that are not available for large growers. Generations of growers pass the old varieties down adapting to the local environment but not available in a seed catalog.

Where do I find local food? I don't know where to begin?

Glad you asked! Farmers' markets and farm stands are the most common locations. There are many websites to help you locate local food across the country, including www.localharvest.org. Local city offices and county extension offices are also reliable sources. Local food is more widely available now in a greater variety of venues. Ask your local grocery store manager if they have local vendors. Ask if your child's school serves local food. Many chefs at your favorite non-franchised restaurants use local foods. There is also an initiative to have local food in hospital food service. See also Part II, "Eat Local".

What do I do with the new kinds of foods I've never seen before?

Farmers who sell the food are the best sources for food preparation tips and they may even have printed recipes to share with you. You can eat many foods raw with little prep other than washing. Your local library has many cookbooks that feature local foods. A wonderful cookbook for beginners is *From Asparagus to Zucchini* published by the Madison Area Community Supported Agriculture Coalition (available at www.eatlocalsimplesteps.com).

Chapter 5:
Getting Started in
Eating Local

As you begin to "eat local," you will become aware of connections – food connections – and this gives you more choices in the foods you eat. You become knowledgeable about the origins of your food, perhaps by talking to a local neighbor who shares from her garden, learning from a farmer whom you meet at the market, or recognizing the land as you pick berries during a walk through the woods. This is not about the food police taking you to task for shopping at the mega mart. It is about becoming aware of how you use your food dollars to support the people and food that benefit you the most. It is about using food dollars to support the people and businesses that reflect your values about food.

What is "local"? There is no established distance for the definition of "local." This may change according to the food that you purchase. We have many cheese factories within 60 miles of my house but the closest place that grows, mills and sells flour is 120 miles away. Our local coffee shop roasts sustainably grown coffee but the beans are from farmers in other countries.

When we are ending our growing season in the upper Midwest, the citrus growers in the South are harvesting their citrus. Local may mean within your county, state or nation. The goal is usually to buy as close as possible, supporting local growers and producers whenever feasible. As you read labels and ask suppliers, you can determine your own definition of local.

Read labels and ask questions. Ask your store produce or dairy manager if there are any locally grown foods stocked or sold under the store label. Check bags, cans or jars for the state or country where your food is produced. Discover the foods grown in your own state and their availability. In our area, for example, potato production is abundant and bags of potatoes carry familiar family names, making it easy to recognize and support our local farmers. Recognizing a company name may simplify your choice – Organic Valley, for instance, is a co-operative of local farmers that produces and sells products in regional areas across the states. The Department of Agriculture website lists the agriculture produced in your state. Ask your county agriculture agent or nutrition extension person about locally produced foods. You may be surprised by the food that is produced close to home.

Start buying local. This may be once per week or a few times per month depending on the availability and your shopping habits. Start with a regular commitment to encourage you and your family to find foods that fit your personal food preferences and budget. Buy during the harvest season when farm stands, farmers' markets  and grocery stores carry local food. If you know a local food grown in your area, commit to buying this food regularly.

Learn the seasons. Each food has a season, despite the year-round supply in your grocery store. In-season foods are much more likely to be locally grown; out-of-season foods are almost certainly shipped long distances. Buying within season assures better quality, including taste and shelf life, and the pleasures of eating will be rewarding when you can take advantage of

the flavors of the harvest. Seasonal eating encourages a variety of foods. Don't worry about eating too many blueberries or figs during the season, since those seasons end and another begins, helping to diversify your diet naturally. You also save money when you buy during peak harvest times.

Visit the farmers' markets regularly. Buying local is convenient when you can shop at a central location with many farmers. If you return often, you begin to recognize both the abundance of food grown in your area and the changing seasons of food. You get to know farmers who can pass along tips for choosing and preparing food. Some may suggest recipes or recommend recipe books.

Experiment with new foods. Along with familiar foods, you begin to recognize and taste new foods. Be adventurous. Give yourself and your family many exposures to the food. Unlike the grocery store, local food sources offer many different varieties of one food, such as peppers, oranges, peaches, etc. Experiment with different types to find your favorite.

Learn to cook, prepare and store local foods. Cooking is an essential skill. You have much more freedom and confidence to prepare local food with a few basic cooking skills. A skillful cook does not need cabinets full of equipment – simple tools such as a knife, cutting board and a few kettles will get you started. Cooking with fresh food is easier since the flavors are much deeper. You do not have to enhance the flavor of fresh food with sauces or spices, making cooking even simpler. Ask the farmer or grocer about storing your food, to maximize the use of any food you buy. Keep some produce, such as tomatoes, potatoes, onions, garlic, at room temperature while others are wrapped and refrigerated. Reduce waste by storing food appropriately.

Simple Steps to Start Eating Local

🍎 Decide on your definition of "local."

🍎 Find food produced and processed locally.

🍎 Start out small with dedicated local purchases each week or month.

🍎 Learn more about the seasonal foods so you can anticipate and plan.

🍎 Find the farmers by visiting markets and farm stands; check out the farm to learn more.

🍎 Experiment with new foods, both raw and cooked.

🍎 Involve your family and friends with trips to the market, potlucks and U-pick adventures.

🍎 Learn to cook.

Chapter 6:
Organic
& Sustainable

We are at a critical juncture in our world where we must recognize the detrimental effects of our current industrial agriculture system and continued overdependence on oil and water. Current food production practices account for 35% of the greenhouse gas emissions contributing to climate change. We are dependent on oil not only for farm machinery and the transportation of food; fertilizer and pesticides are also derived from oil. Water is used not only to extract oil but also to irrigate crops. In both instances we are not tracking the amount of water that is being used, but we do know that water is being displaced and we are not recharging our ground water. The increased dependence on chemical inputs is also polluting our water. Healthy soil and diversity of plant protects not only soil but water. History shows that we are most successful when we work with, rather than against, nature.

You are one of the many who are redirecting the food system to connect land, farmer and consumer. By purchasing local foods, and choosing neighborhood farmers who support organic and sustainable agriculture production, you are supporting food choices that assure we are eating well, sustaining ourselves without compromising our children's future and keeping farmers in business to secure a food supply.

Organic Agriculture

While "conventional farming" (with chemical pesticides, insecticides and fertilizers) constitutes the majority of food production, organic production has steadily increased, with acreage increasing by 15% annually between 2002 and 2008. Organic agriculture relies on maintaining healthy plants and animals by understanding the natural cycles and conditions.  We reduce or eliminate chemicals when we maintain healthy foundations of agriculture: soil, water and plants.

Nature promotes smorgasbords, not supersizing. Land in nature demonstrates diversity. The diversity above the soil helps maintain the diversity below and vice versa. Biodiversity in an area keeps balance with weeds and predators controlled, so chemicals are not required. Healthy soil produces healthy plants. Healthy soil also takes carbon from the atmosphere, called carbon sequestering, and absorbs water which protects both air and water.

Maintaining biodiversity of crops assures a genetic stock for different growing, weather and soil conditions, especially important when we think about climate change. Farmers have always been the seed cultivators: Farmers and gardeners create new types of plants. Supporting seed saving, small seed companies and farmers who use

heritage stock will keep a diverse variety in our food supply, and buying locally will keep diversity specialized to our specific geographic areas intact as many heritage plants and animals are only available locally. See chapter 35 for more specifics about choosing organic.

Sustainable Food System

When organic agriculture began to grow in the 1970s, it brought renewed attention to farming methods that decrease chemical inputs and support economic parity and social justice. Sustainable agriculture pays attention to natural resources and people involved in the food system so that safe, affordable food is available to everyone at a fair price. It implies planning for generations of farming and eating.

Biodynamic farming looks at the whole area of land, both cultivated and not cultivated, to understand the relationship between plants, trees, soil, insects, animals and humans. Understanding the connectedness of all living systems helps us maintain production without harm. We can use our curiosity and science to be innovative and work with nature rather than attempt to control or conquer. In a biodynamic system, farmers produce as many food needs as possible within the farm system rather than just one crop. The integration of many living systems is successful because one system benefits another. For instance, intercropping flowers attracts insects which also pollinate plants; intercropping plants between rows protects soil erosion and maintains moisture, and diversified farms produce more per acre than monocropped farms.

The future of our food is assured when farming as a profession secures a livable wage, agriculture protects our natural resources; consumers have nourishing, affordable food, and communities have a reliable local food system. A sustainable food system is an accountable food system, and challenges every citizen to take an active part by voting with our forks.

Chapter 7: Seasonal Eating

Our family's first shock with seasonal eating came after joining a Community Supported Agriculture (CSA) farm. As members, we received a box of produce each week. We all awaited eagerly for the tomatoes which we knew were coming and continued to wait through weeks of radishes, peas, salad greens, spinach, eggplant, carrots and the list continues. Halfway through the season, the tomatoes finally arrived. Learning about the abundance and flow of food made us realize that you cannot rush a tomato. We learned that seasonal eating means to be aware of the growing season of different foods, to know how to prepare them and to be open to trying new foods.

After that first year, we relaxed into the bounty of the seasons, experimenting with new recipes, learning to identify new leafy greens, tomatillos and celeriac and other new tastes and textures. Seasonal eating became a surprise box with beautiful colors and scents and an air of mystery, since we could not fully anticipate the juncture of rain, temperature and soil conditions with weekly accuracy. This anticipation made us appreciate the weekly harvest all the more. After having our fill of salad greens for three weeks, we were happy when the heat ended their reign and the next crop began.

Monoeating is the continuous eating of the same foods – people often do this unconsciously. We typically eat the same type of foods for breakfast, whether a wheat product such as bread or cereal, and repeat similar patterns for lunch as a sandwich, fruit and vegetable. Seasonal eating gives short spurts of monoeating – usually no more than two to three weeks; then the weather changes or rainfall patterns shift  and we are ready for the next crop. Seasonal eating assures that we vary our meals regularly since nature changes throughout the growing season. Following the seasons does not imply that only one crop is available; rather, groups of crops dominate, slowly leaving as the next group gains in productivity.

You can find charts or lists of seasonal foods at many local offices or organizations such as your county extension office, Department of Agriculture and local food groups – these are often available at your local library. Also, check online resources for local foods in your area such as the "Seasonal Food Guide" at www.eatwell.org.

Visiting the farmers' markets on a weekly basis alerts you to seasonal produce, which may be surprising when we have been accustomed to a small, consistent year-round supply in the grocery stores.  Many commonly eaten items that store well are seasonal, such as root crops, maple syrup, honey, nuts, seeds, and beans.

"Tomatoes in January" are the best known example of the confusion surrounding seasonality of food and illustrates the compromises necessary to have these available during Wisconsin's cold, northern climate. Tomatoes are always in season somewhere in the world, but they are harvested while unripe and hard, and flown or trucked thousands of miles to our stores, then gassed to "ripen". Not only do these tomatoes undercut the local agriculture in other countries, but they waste valuable fuel to get to our plates, compromising our future resources.

Adjusting meal planning to coincide with seasonal foods is easy with a few simple changes. The first simple step is to add ingredients to your mainstay dishes and meals. Fruits and vegetables make easy snacks, side dishes or quick additions. A soup, casserole or stir-fry dish can have a fresh taste and look with the produce that you find in the farmers' market. As the season unfolds, plan your menu around the available foods.

Next, experiment with the different varieties of the same food; you may have noticed that there are different types of potatoes, plums, peaches or squashes in your area. Each choice offers a slightly different color, flavor or texture to your foods. As you shop locally, you soon discover your favorites. Many of these are heritage crops or small production crops, exclusively available from your farmers since grocery stores cannot offer this wide range and varieties. Heritage crops are known for taste, rather than attributes that make them easier to transport.

Local chefs, authors, restaurants and organizations are increasingly focused on local seasonal eating and offer tips on incorporating these into your cooking and eating. Other opportunities to focus on and learn about local food include chef demonstrations in farmers' markets, restaurant menu selections with advertised local food, and cooking classes that emphasize seasonal choices. Our local June sustainable living fair sells food with a seasonal twist, so the salsa and sandwich toppings vary by the food available during the preceding days – pizza toppings, for instance, include local greens and garlic scapes while desserts feature just-picked strawberries.

Regional cookbooks with recipes arranged by season are also readily available. These make shopping at farmers' markets easy, since the majority of ingredients in each recipe is ready for harvest at the same time. Seasonal foods naturally complement each other. Ask your local farmer for cooking tips and recipe suggestions.

Ask your produce manager about seasonal foods – chances are, they are the ones with sale prices. Be sure to check the label or tags for the origin of produce. Local produce is not always clearly advertised so some sleuthing on your part is necessary.

Simple Steps to Seasonal Eating

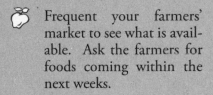 Frequent your farmers' market to see what is available. Ask the farmers for foods coming within the next weeks.

Find the season for your favorite foods; try new foods in the meantime.

Check out seasonal cookbooks from the library and bookstore. Buying seasonal foods is easier when your ingredients match the season.

Chapter 8:
First Steps:
Healthy Eating &
Cooking

Our eating habits are constantly changing with our palates adjusting to new tastes and our lifestyles influencing food choices. Currently, if your food is mostly processed, packaged food, then changing to healthier eating is a transition for your palate as well as your pocketbook – so be patient with yourself and others as you change shopping, cooking and eating habits. Instead of being restrictive, local eating expands your world as you enjoy the food and support the producers around you. Changing to a more local diet is an adventure that will increase your health, expand your choices and help save the environment. You can begin with these simple steps.

Take an inventory. Before making any changes, carefully look at what you and your family are currently eating at home, work, school and leisure. Where do you currently purchase these foods and where could you purchase foods in the future? Think about the values that you have about your food and whether your current food habits support these values for you and your family. If not, then you may prioritize changes by importance and ease to make the transition enjoyable and worthwhile. See Section II, "Eat Local, Finding Local Food" to help find where your local food is marketed.

Reduce processed and packaged foods. One simple step for healthier eating is to take control of your food. Knowledgeable shoppers know when to use processed and packaged foods to their advantage rather than be influenced by market-ing and sales. You get more for your food dollar and have more control over your food by reducing packaged and processed foods in your diet, realizing that each processing step eliminates nutrients, and each ingredient that is added eliminates the control you have over your food. Un-processed foods do not have salt, sugar, fat or flavorings added which means you control what you are eating. Single items such as canned beans or bulk packages of pasta or rice are a bet-ter value and give you more flexibility and control.

Adjust your palate. If your palate is trained for the high sugar, salt and chem-ical tastes of processed foods, changing to a fresh diet requires a period of ad-justment. Unwittingly, your taste buds recognize high levels of salt or sugar that have been increasing in processed foods in recent years. Since salt enhances other flavors, eating foods with less salt will, initially, taste flat – so allow weeks for taste buds to adjust to reduced levels in your food. Experiment with fresh herbs and spices to add flavor and gradually reduce salt. Ripe or dried fruits will help during this transition since their natural sweetness and flavors enhance taste. After this weaning period, you will find that many foods have more complex tastes and subtle flavors while enjoying a level of salt and sweetness that is complimentary.

Save time and money by shopping local first. Simplifying our food choices and shopping for local food increases the variety of our meals, inexpensively and healthfully, without having to devote time and energy to shopping and complicated meal preparation. We can go to the garden, open the Community Supported Agriculture (CSA) box or buy our weekly produce from the farmers' market to add interest and variety. A few staples at the grocery store have eliminated shopping time and the temptation to buy foods based on coupons or marketing schemes.

Substitute fresh and raw. A simple first step is having abundant raw fruits and vegetables available and eliminating the need to cook. You and your family can increase your consumption of fruits and vegetables easily by displaying fruit in a bowl  that is on the table; placing trimmed vegetables on the top shelf of the refrigerator; or packing snacks in lunches the previous night — this tempts everyone to grab and go. By substituting these prepared fresh foods into your cooking, you will have easy ingredients readily available which simplifies your cooking.

Use less but good quality. Given the current obesity crisis, we know there is not a deficit of calories in our diets, so we can be confident that choosing foods of higher quality, flavor and value rather than foods with high fat and sugar but few nutrients will meet our basic needs and be more satisfying. In short, more is not always better if it compromises our health and well-being and our children's future. Good eating comes from paying attention to the food while we eat, appreciating flavorful food, enjoying the social aspects of a meal and eating only until we are 80% full.

Food with complex flavor comes from whole foods since nature provides abundant flavor compounds, detected when we smell, cook and eat real food. Much of the local food available directly from farmers is not only better quality but often a better value for your dollar. Some local foods may be more expensive but provide intense flavor; often these foods are used in smaller quantities. Fresh garlic stores well and comes in a variety of flavors and intensities in the farmers' market. The price per pound may seem prohibitive but remember that you buy a bulb of garlic that has many cloves and may have a more intense flavor so you can use a small amount. If you choose to use animal products, you can disperse the flavor throughout the dish by cutting into small pieces and adding to a larger combination of beans or grains. Stronger flavored cheeses such as those that are aged will add more flavor to a dish so you can use judiciously.

Cook gently and efficiently. Steaming, stir-frying and poaching are quick cooking techniques that save time and fuel. For all of these, the peeling and chopping takes less time than cooking. We may unnecessarily remove peels or stalks and unwittingly reduce nutrients and flavor.  For instance, valuable nutrients are in and just underneath the skin in a potato so peeling wastes nutrients, including valuable fiber. If you are worried about chemicals, then ask the farmer if pesticides or other chemicals were used in the production or choose organic foods to reduce the chemical load of your food. Remember that children can help with the first easy steps of cleaning and preparing the vegetables. This teaches valuable life skills and gives you family time.

Vegetables and grains can retain the maximum flavor and color with steaming. Add a minimal amount of water to the bottom of the pan, cover and use low heat. Since steaming cooks food very fast, check frequently. Another time saving trick is to soak grains or beans overnight or in the morning before work and you will reduce cooking time for dinner.

Easy cooking will help you incorporate whole foods without complicating schedules. A basic formula in our house is to have pasta, rice or potatoes as a base; stir-fry or steam seasonal vegetables; add one or more types of beans; play with flavorings such as basil, thyme or oregano for Mediterranean flavor, or ginger, garlic, onion for more Asian flavor; and add liquid to adjust the moisture. This meal takes about 20 minutes to prepare and varies with seasonal food choices. Another quick meal is to add a combination of these ingredients in a slow cooker. Roasting squash, vegetables, potatoes and garlic, then adding cheese or beans is easy and convenient.

There are many recipe books available in your library or bookstore that provide simple cooking techniques, focus on the local, seasonal foods in the ingredient list and provide guides to purchasing or cooking for different produce. A popular cookbook that does all of this is *From Asparagus to Zucchini* cookbook published by the Madison Area Community Supported Agriculture Coalition, www.macsac.org.

Simple Steps to Healthy Eating & Cooking

- Eat more whole foods; reduce processed and ready to eat foods.

- Eat plant based foods, especially fruits, vegetables and whole grains.

- Eat with the seasons for maximum taste, flavor and variety.

- Use simple ingredients in different ways.

- Use gentle cooking techniques such as steaming or poaching.

- Use herbs and spices for flavor and health benefits.

- Eat quality food in small quantities rather than more food of low quality.

Chapter 9:
For the Children
(and Ourselves)

School food, despite being the brunt of jokes, has provided millions of meals to children over decades. I still remember the homemade creamed tuna over biscuits at my high school as a highlight. One recent evening, I attended a talk about food served in the schools. The talk featured a panel of school food directors who spoke about challenges with nourishing our children. They described their efforts to change school lunch offerings from processed foods (high in fat, sodium and sugar while low in fiber and nutrients) to whole foods. One director recounted standing by the lunchroom waste receptacle, watching children throw away baked potatoes at the end of the meal. She asked the children why they had not eaten their food. The answers ranged from "I don't know," to "It takes too long," and "I don't know what it is." The lunchroom volunteers come on baked potato day to teach the children how to put the toppings into the potato and eat it. Since we process most potatoes that children eat nowadays, children need coaching to eat a baked potato!

Children, too often, are simply are not familiar with food – their sustenance. This is often because we are not teaching them about food at home or within our communities. Rather than consume food, we eat  *food products* that may have come from a plant or animal at one time, but are barely recognizable as anything from *nature*. Today, our children are losing much more than the knowledge of eating a baked potato.

Food nourishes our bodies, and our food choices often are a reflection of our cultural food heritage, influenced by those foods that were available to our parents and grandparents. Cultural foods include the seeds carried by our immigrant families, the favorite recipes for celebrations, and the symbolic foods of our religious history. Food supports our values of nourishment, not only of body but also of spirit.

I travel around the country talking about food and nutrition, and in my workshops, I ask participants to list the food values which they would like their children and grandchildren to hold. These important values most often include: eating with family and friends; eating unprocessed, whole foods fresh from the  land; recognizing who grows our food and how it is grown; and knowing family food traditions, such as specific foods and recipes, traditional ways of celebrating, cooking techniques, and knowledge about gardening and preserving. After we talk about our food values, I ask people to reflect on where our children would observe and experience this. I am interested in knowing how our children will learn these values, whose legacy and survival are so important to us. If the family, school, church or community settings are not reflecting and reinforcing the food values we cherish, then we need to consider the current food values that our children are learning.

When we eat together, we create food memories by exposing children to new foods, teaching how to eat foods, deciding when to eat foods, demonstrating where to eat and letting children determine how much to eat. How do we eat with a fork, chopsticks, or our fingers? Should we eat in the kitchen, the car, the living room, or standing at the counter? How many times should we chew our food? How do we prepare our food? Where does our food come from? What are the seasons of food? What food do we eat regularly, occasionally, seldom, or never? Has anyone in our family grown their own food? What were grocery stores like a generation ago? What foods are part of our heritage and our grandparents' heritage? Are these foods still available? What new foods have immigrants brought us?

Families, including children, have power over their food choices when they are familiar with food. When we allow food manufacturers and grocery stores to decide our food system, then we lose the heritage of food, dismantle family farms and relegate food to filling our stomachs. Everyone surrounding a child models food values and votes with their forks. If we visit the local farmers' market and talk with a farmer who grows our food, our children recognize this farmer's importance in connecting our food with the land in our community. If we make meal time a priority, no matter how simple the meal, we teach the social value of food. If we eat fresh, whole food with awareness, then we are creating food memories that our senses remember for decades. Reclaiming our food heritage from our parents and grandparents engenders a strong connection to both food and family.

Simple Steps for Teaching Children

Model the food values you want passed onto children. Adults give subtle cues to children when we appreciate food, know local farmers, or enjoy cooking. It is our responsibility, not only as parents but also as adults within communities, to support food values.

Explore the origins of food. Farmers' markets, CSA farms, cheese factories, U-pick days and gardening are some of the avenues for discovering where your food originates. The sight, sound, and smell of food intrigues children with enticing tastes such as a heritage tomato fresh from the vine. When children are in my garden, they are happy to snack as we pluck a fresh pea off the vine or a blueberry from the bush; surprised to unearth potatoes or carrots from under the ground; or amazed to see honey in the combs.

Support food education in schools. Some families in your community cannot afford a wide variety of foods, but as a community, we can support wholesome foods in our schools, reinforcing our food values while ensuring that all children receive fresh,  healthy, delicious food. Food service directors, teachers and administrators need our encouragement to maintain school as a learning environment about food and healthy eating.

Adults need to be in charge. As fussy as children may be, adults are responsible for children in our world. Adults decide the food environment; this includes the types of foods offered, as well as when, where, and how food is consumed. While children decide how much they eat, parents are responsible for the foods that are available.

Explore new foods. Humans, by nature, are afraid of what is new, so introduce food multiple times to your family. It may take fifteen to twenty exposures before your family decides whether they enjoy new tastes such as celeriac, pummelos or tatsoi. If you want your children to try new foods, continue tasting them frequently over weeks or months – exposure makes a difference.

Involve children in food activities. When children are involved in growing or preparing their food, they are more likely to try it. Children can grow vegetables in pots, add ingredients, toss the salad, set the table and/or tidy up. Shopping at the farmers' market is often a child's favorite activity. Frequently including children in food activities increases their willingness to eat a variety of foods.

Section II

Eat Local: Finding Local Food

Chapter 10: The Grocery Store Challenge

Finding local where you shop

Grocery stores may span from small, independently owned single stores to large national chain megastores. Each store has its benefits and challenges for local food. Since the majority of shoppers spend a significant portion of their food dollars at the grocery store, consumers and farmers alike enjoy stores that provide local food options. The most compelling reason is the convenience of "one-stop" shopping. Many consumers prefer to spend their time and fuel most efficiently in shopping by finding most of their purchases within a small geographic area.

The grocery store is not only a place for food but also a place to socialize: We see our neighbors, friends and their children at these stores. Grocery stores are often places where high school students are first employed and learn customer service skills. In our family, several of my children had their first jobs at grocery stores and moved up to other positions. All of this familiarity between the employees and customers builds loyalty and community.

In return, the community develops a trust that the grocery store owner has some loyalty to the community. Our stores are often major donors of both food and money to various community functions such as day-old bakery items donated to food shelters and sponsors of the soccer league. Whether the store is independently owned or a national chain, the customers and employees are from the same community, and collaborating with local farmers is a natural fit for these stores.

Grocers like to capture as much of the consumer's dollars by offering as many products as possible. Once a customer is within the store, owners hope customers will stay and shop for all their needs. The rising demand for local food has resulted in opportunities to attract and keep customers. Stores are increasing their selection of local foods and farmer's markets are starting in their parking lots; both offer the convenience of local foods.

Check labels. Local produce may be available but not clearly advertised as local, so check labels and ask managers for local products to help you identify these. Recently, I found local Wisconsin apples next to the Washington apples. The small tag that closes the bag had the name and place of the apple grower – had I not looked, I would have easily missed these. In my area grocery stores, many local dairy products are available, including award-winning cheeses. A local coffee roaster also has shelf space in a few of our stores. Local food includes both fresh and value-added foods displayed in various places throughout the store.

Customer loyalty. Your opinion and your dollars matter to grocery store owners. If your grocery store is an independently owned store or a small grocery chain, store managers often respond quickly to requests, since the decisions for inventory involve fewer people and you are able to speak directly to the person who orders the food. These stores require a smaller inventory to maintain, making it easier for farmers to supply the amount of fresh food needed. Small stores are more dependent on their fewer customers and therefore likely to respond to their requests and able to offer a more specialized, personal service. So don't hesitate to ask for local food and encourage your family and friends to do likewise.

The larger the grocery store chain, the less influence an individual customer has. Corporate headquarters and regional offices make decisions about store products, organization, service, etc. and trucks transport products from central warehouses. These stores follow national or regional trends more often than local requests. The local manager may have less flexibility for new products, unless a greater number of customers make requests. A recent example is Wal-Mart, which has begun supplying local produce in some of their area stores, as regional popularity and demand for these increases.

Shopping Recommendations

Scan your favorite grocery store for local products. Managers will be able to describe the local food currently available, seasonal trends in buying local, requirements for buying local and favored delivery methods. Encourage grocers to identify local producers with large signs or have a designated local food section. Check labels to identify the producer and ask the manager which food products are local. Notice that for some products that are already frozen or canned, labels may indicate the company that distributed or manufactured the product rather than who grew the food. Become familiar with local company names to help you choose quickly.

Talk with the store manager and department managers. There is no accepted definition for local so distances from farm to store may vary. Grocery stores must be able to have products on a regular cycle so buying within the state or multi-state region rather than nationally may help them guarantee supply and identify local products. It may be easier for stores to work with distributors who already have a relationship with regional farmers rather than with new, individual farmers. Frequent conversations with store managers encourage both you and the manager to locate local foods. Please compliment managers on their efforts to make local food available.

Investigate other area grocery stores, co-ops or natural food stores for local products. Talk with these store managers for suggestions on getting local food in your neighborhood store. They may be able to offer useful strategies to help your neighborhood store transition to more local food.

Supplying information to your neighborhood store will make it easier for the manager to follow-up with your request. If you know a farmer who is selling at another store, talk to the farmer about contacting your neighborhood store manager. Farmers plan their production based on market demand, so the farmer may not have produced enough food to supply many area stores this season, but may be able to grow more for the following year. Follow-up with the store manager and farmer – it may take a few seasons to establish the relationship between grower and store manager.

Become knowledgeable about the foods produced abundantly in your area. Fresh foods have seasonal cycles or need to be processed (dried, canned, frozen) for year-round availability. Suggest a specific food that you know is in large supply, such as pumpkins or oranges. The manager may be willing to first try local foods on an occasional basis. Encourage family and friends to buy these new foods and compliment the manager for his efforts.

Many foods have a long storage life: root crops such as potatoes, onions, squash, and garlic can be stored for months; fruits such as grapefruits, apples and figs keep for long periods and have extended seasons. Other foods may need minimal processing such as dried fruit or mushrooms. Store managers may be willing to try a local food with a longer shelf life so there is less pressure to sell immediately and less money lost with spoilage. Customers also appreciate buying local food that will keep for weeks.

Consider value added foods that are local. Value added foods are processed in some way to promote long shelf life, including jams, jellies, relishes, pickles, etc. This processing takes place in a commercial facility that meets strict safety codes. Many communities are building commercial kitchen and processing centers, then renting space and equipment to small processors. Many different foods are available in every section of your store, including family recipes for canned items. Look for juices, ciders and milk bottled nearby. We have a small business that bottles dairy in returnable glass bottles and distributes to small grocers. My friend sells  popular fresh salsa to area grocers. Dried fruit, herbs and spices may be available; honey and maple syrups produced from local trees and flowers are common. Local bakeries may have a small shelf space. We even have a local potato chip factory in our city. Supporting these products help small entrepreneurs as well as farmers. Many entrepreneurs, such as Ben & Jerry's ice cream, started as local food entrepreneurs.

Shelf space in a store requires a slotting fee. Small producers may work with a regional distributor so there are a variety of products available for stores. These distributors may have a distinct label or store section such as "Made in Vermont". The distributors keep the farm description and stories that customers seek but also  help farmers in readying the product for commercial markets by negotiating prices, entering the product into a store's computer system, and arranging delivery schedules. These may be cost and time prohibitive for an individual farmer but reasonable for small distributors that work with many farmers. The identity of the farmer is available for the consumer and the store manager can work easily with the distributor to meet the store needs.

You vote with your dollars each time your put something in your grocery cart. You can use this purchasing power and your relationship with your neighborhood grocer to support local food in stores that are convenient for you.

Questions to Ask Grocery Store Managers

- What local foods are currently available? Does this change throughout the year?

- Do you, or will you, clearly label or identify local food for consumers?

- Can these foods be advertised as "local" or "regional" within the stores or in-store flyers?

- Are employees knowledgeable about local food sources and encouraged to promote these?

- Which local foods could be added? Seasonal local produce such as onions, apples, potatoes, dairy, cheese, etc.? Is a processed item more likely (frozen or canned)?

- How can I help locate a farmer or promote a new local food?

Chapter 11: How to Pick Produce

Produce is among the most enticing food, with bright colors, crisp textures and juicy interiors. The abundant variety of fruits and vegetables makes choosing ripe food an enticing adventure. Finding the perfect peach or melon is rewarding in its succulence, but it can also be a disappointment if you spend money for produce that is either too young or ripe. The farmer or grocery produce staff will be happy to help guide you in your selections. There are a few general suggestions for choosing delicious produce.

Healthy eaters consume as many colors in the week as possible, try to eat the colors of the rainbow during the week. As you enter the farmers' market or grocery store, notice all the different colors and possibilities. Different colors provide different phytochemicals (beneficial plant chemicals) and nutrient mixes. Buy in small quantities: large quantity purchases are not the best investment of your food dollar if it leads to boring eating and increased spoilage. The farmers' market, especially in peak season, reflects the most abundance for your local area.

No perfect produce. Unlike the grocery store, where there are limited varieties of produce which are selected for uniformity, local food reflects nature and the fact that living produce varies from one item to another, however slightly. Learn to tolerate imperfections and recognize a skin blemish from damaged produce. Food grown commercially is wasted when the market only tolerates cosmetically perfect produce.

Freshness counts. The best value for your produce is to buy at peak freshness. In general, fresh produce is firm or slightly yielding while very firm, and soft produce may indicate under- or overripe. Many fruits and vegetables start losing moisture, flavor and aroma after being picked. Generally bright colors indicate good quality but this may vary with the specific variety of a produce. I grow a variety of tomatoes that stay green while ripe rather than transition to red. Peaches may be white or yellow while figs come in a variety of colors. Your farmer can explain the differences between different varieties of the same type of fruit or vegetable.

Variety matters. Every kind of fruit or vegetable has a number of varietals; you are probably familiar with apple varieties such as Granny Smith, Delicious or Braeburn. Differences may vary by color, aroma, taste, or texture; cooking and storage qualities can also differ. Unfortunately, with the trend towards large farming, central distribution and grocers, varietals have been disappearing. We have lost 6,000 varieties of apples in the last century, largely because of narrow commercial production and retailing. An advantage of supporting local food is access to these varietals that do not ship well or are not produced in enough quantity to ship, making these local treasures. These heirlooms are typically found in farmers' markets, where the vendors are usually experts about the characteristics of a variety and will often let you taste before you buy. They can also give you handling tips for each variety.

Ask about production. Organic production prohibits chemical pesticides and genetically modified produce. For non-organic produce, inquire out about any chemicals, waxes or preservatives that were added to the fruits and vegetables during production and write down the name of any unfamiliar chemicals to look up later. Ask the farmer why they use any additives; the more you know, the more confident you can be about your produce. You are also alerting farmers that you prefer food without these chemicals.

Consider price. The best value for your dollar is the freshest vegetables and fruits that you can eat before spoiling. The beginning of the farmers' market day or the produce delivery day in your grocery store will have the best selection with the freshest produce possible, but you can also get bargains at the end of the farmers' market on fresh produce that the farmer would rather sell than carry home. The fresher the produce, (closer the food is to harvest), the longer the food will last in your home, so ask when the food was picked to determine how long it will last. Produce with a higher water content, such as salad greens, berries or cucurbits, needs to be eaten quickly, whereas starchier foods such as storage crops (potatoes, squash, onions, etc.), can be kept for weeks and months. Buying smaller quantities also helps you choose more variety.

Follow your senses. Use all of your senses in choosing produce. Color, smell, feel and heft can indicate the best fruit. Check for any bruises, molds, or cuts; feel for any sliminess or shriveling, too soft or too hard; and smell for off-odors such as mold or overripe. What follows is a general guide for choosing categories of vegetables and fruits.

Vegetables

Alliums (garlic, leeks, onions, shallots, scallions). Stalks should be fresh without wilting or discoloration at the tips; bulbs have a smooth skin without cracks or nicks.

Amaranth or Beet family (amaranth, beet, chard, spinach). The greens should be bright and lush without wilting or sliminess; bulbs are firm with an earthy smell.

Aster or Sunflower family (artichokes, cardoons, endive, escarole, lettuce, radicchio, Jerusalem artichokes or sun chokes) should have leaves that look fresh and stand upright rather than wilted and bent. They should have a firm texture, as if you were handling a bouquet of flowers. Avoid leaves that look discolored or damaged, especially on the tips and whole, unbroken leaves.

Brassica or cruciferous vegetables (arugula, bok choy, broccoli, brussel sprouts, cabbage, cauliflower, kale, kohlrabi, radish, rapini, rutabaga, tat soi, turnip). Greens will be bright and turgid rather than limp and without discoloration or broken leaves. The bulbs will be closed heads with firm texture.

Cucurbits (cucumber, chayote, melon, pumpkin, squash, watermelon). Smooth skinned, slightly to moderately firm. Skin should be without bruises, soft areas, or mold.

Legumes (beans, peas, fava beans, soybeans, lentils). Look for crisp pods, fairly straight with no cuts or holes. The skin is fairly smooth.

Nightshades (eggplant, potato, tomato, pepper). The skin is smooth and unbroken, there is firmness to the flesh rather than wrinkled indicating moisture.

Umbelliferae (carrot, celery, fennel, parsnip). Flesh is firm, without cracks or holes. The leaves at the top should be crisp and upright rather than limp.

Fruits

Stone fruit (apricot, cherry, plum, peach, pluot, nectarine). These fruits are lightly soft, no bruising, perfumed, sweet fragrance. The skin should be intact without soft areas or bruising.

Pomes (apple, chokeberry, juneberry, loquat, medlar, pomegranate, pear quince, rowan, service tree). These fruits have firm but not hard flesh without bruises or holes, some scabbing is fine, ripe fragrance, no discoloration in the skin color.

Berries (blackberry, raspberry, cloudberry, wineberry, bearberry, bilberry, blueberry, cranberry, huckleberry, lingonberry, barberry, currant, elderberry, gooseberry, honeysuckle, nannyberry, wolfberry, crowberry, mulberry). Fruit is lightly firm and succulent rather than shrunken and limp, check for complete color; uncrushed berries; ripe fragrance, no mold.

Mediterranean origin fruits (fig, grape, jujube, black mulberry, pomegranate, date palm). Colors vary with variety so know the bright color of your local fruit to determine ripeness, slight

A wonderful resource that gives shopping tips on produce, including picture and information about storing, peak season, nutrition, and serving ideas can be found at the California Department of Health Champions for Change website:

http://www.cachampionsforchange.net/en/Produce-Quick-Tips.php

There are also a growing number of apps for your iphone that you can take with you to the farmer's market and grocery store.

softness but not firm or mushy; heaviness may also indicate ripeness.

Citrus fruits (citron, grapefruit, key lime, kumquat, lemon, lime, mandarin, orange, ugli fruit). Fruit is firm and heavy for its size with a sweet, fresh fragrance; no mold or soft spots on flesh which is free from cuts or scratches. Color is not indicative of maturity since cold temperature affects color, rather than maturity. Unlike stone fruits, citrus fruits must be ripe when picked as they will not ripen with storage so they must be picked ripe.

Simple Steps to Picking Produce

- Look for vibrant colors. Chose a variety of colors to eat throughout the week for best health benefits.

- Smell for the cleanest, freshest fragrance without any moldy or off-smells.

- Look for intact skin; discard any fruit or vegetables that have bruises, soft spots, cracks, holes or slimy leaves.

- Learn about new varietals from the farmer or produce manager. Locally grown foods may offer heritage varieties not possible in the larger chain markets.

- Be adventurous! Try new fruits or vegetables each time you shop. Experiment with adding produce in different ways, both raw and cooked, into your meals.

Chapter 12:

Questions to Ask Your Produce Manager

With the increased popularity of the local foods, there is a high probability that local produce is in your grocery store at least part of the year. Our neighborhood produce manager has been very receptive to sourcing local foods and you may find a similarly friendly person. The more familiar you are with the produce manager, the better informed you can be about how the store sources its produce and possibilities for increasing local food in your favorite grocery store.

Know the manager. The first step is to introduce yourself to the produce manager and discuss your interest in local foods and your preference to purchase produce grown by your area farmers as much as possible. The produce staff may already be knowledgeable about local produce and can talk to you about who grew the food, the seasonality of the local produce and frequency of local shipments to the store. Your conversations with the produce staff will alert them to your interests and increase their knowledge of local food. It is the produce manager who ultimately controls the supply of food so you want to encourage the manager to find local produce.

Buy local now. What local produce is available? Grocers are able to stock some local food year-round, even in the northern states that have freezing temperatures, thanks to innovative tunnel

farming throughout the winter. New regulations require country of origin labeling for all produce which helps narrow your search. The country, state or region is indicated on bag labels, stickers, tag closures or bulk display signs. For produce grown
in your state, ask the manager if he knows the specific area of production or farmer who grew it. The local produce may be sold under the brand name of the store; identifying local produce from your area farms is often confusing without talking to the staff. Thank the manager for supporting local farmers and remind him of your interest in buying local.

Advertise local. Do they – or will they – display local and increase signage? Often, the produce section has local produce but it is not widely advertised. Just recently, I was surprised to find local potatoes next to the Idaho ones; the back label alerted me to my local farmer. Occasionally, the name of the farm is listed. When finding local produce, ask the manager to advertise local produce with large signs and keep produce sorted accordingly. Since the definition for local may vary, our local food co-op marks food with a tag that indicates the distance from farm to store, helping customers decide how local they choose to purchase.

Increase local foods. Frequent requests get more local produce in our grocery stores; involve organizations to lobby for local. Partner with environmental or religious groups to support local food. Since produce has a short shelf life, managers are happy to accommodate customers if they know the product will move quickly and not spoil. Find out what barriers there are for having more local produce and try to help eliminate these.

Questions to Ask Produce Managers

What foods are currently stocked that are local? How does the store define "local" vendors?

If local foods are not currently stocked, is local and organic produce available?

If local foods are currently stocked, what is needed to increase the local produce or add "local and organic" choices in the store?

Which local foods could be added? Seasonal local produce such as onions, apples, potatoes, etc.?

Where are the local foods grown? A map in the store with farm locations is welcomed by consumers.

How fast between the farm field and the grocery store? How often is the produce delivered?

Can the local foods be labeled or identified for consumers?

Can these foods be more prominently displayed?

Can these foods be included as "local" or "regional" in advertising, both in-store and other media?

Do you have any suggestions for cooking the local produce? Recipes?

Can you help feature a local farmer and have a store tasting?

Would the store sponsor a chef demonstration that features a local food?

If your community has harvest celebrations, ask the produce manager to participate with local food specials.

Chapter 13:
Farmers' Markets

The best place for fresh, healthy food – other than your own backyard – is directly from the farmer, and the first place to start is the farmers' market. Farmers' markets are expanding across the country and they are one of the most active places in a community. The number of farmers' markets has increased each year since 1995 and now there are more than 16,000 farmers' markets across the country. Farmers are making it more convenient to connect directly with their customers.

Farmers' markets not only provide an outlet for food but are wonderful social hubs of activity. Many farmers' markets create a semi-structured atmosphere with tables and tents. Some markets may be permanent buildings or shelters while others may be temporary tables or booths in a parking lot or street. Markets may have as few as two or three farmers in one small area or enough to span an entire parking lot. The market is the time to talk about food and farming with the people who know best, the farmers.

The "one-stop shop" for fresh food. If you want the best food for the best price, then the farmers' market is the most convenient, one-stop for shopping. Farmers harvest close to sale time so the food has maximum nutrition at peak flavor. Markets also offer the most variety of foods that changes throughout the seasons so you can shop frequently and try different foods. To save money, buy small quantities of various items and return often.

The farmers' market usually provides a number of different foods and products. The type of market reflects food that can be grown in your area and the cultural preferences. For instance, in our local upper Midwest market we have a growing season from June until October and a winter market that follows. We have a traditionally northern European population who immigrated from Poland and Germany with more recent Mexican and Thai families moving into our area. Our market, in its most abundant months, is a wonderful mix of tomatoes, peppers, garlic, as well as tomatillos, lemongrass, and Thai basil. Not only can we buy the foods that we were familiar with as children, but we have the opportunity to taste the foods of other cultures.

More than food. Farmers' markets often have prepared as well as fresh foods and other goods, and the variety from one market to the other is often incredible (and delightful!). One market I visited in Iowa had fresh produce, meats and honey as well as wines, jams, jellies and bakery. Booths were selling smoothies, wraps, rice and sauces, tortillas and enchiladas. Crafts and artwork were also for sale and a local knife company had a display table. The Saturday market spanned several downtown city blocks that were closed to traffic for the morning. Street musicians and children's activities are also very common in weekend markets. The market was full of people with bags, wagons and small baskets.

While at the market be sure to ask for other upcoming activities. Each month during the summer, we have a guest chef who demonstrates a new dish using ingredients available during that day, and then distributes recipes. Communities have concerts, special activities for children, art events, and other events that make farmers' markets popular for entertainment.

Your first visit to a farmers' market may be overwhelming. These tips may help you be ready for your first adventure. The market products change throughout the season and the number of vendors may vary during the week, ask the farmers if you do not see a food you enjoy and return often.

Simple Steps Before Going to the Market

- *Check locations of the markets you plan to visit.* Often farmers' markets are only in a location on specified days of the week or times; cities may have more than one market. Verify location and time each year, for markets may relocate.

- *Market timings.* Go early if you want shop with less people and get the first picks. Note limited hours of markets during the week.

- *Bring small bills and change.* Often, vendors do cash-only business. Some vendors are able to take credit cards or electronic balance transfer (EBT) cards, but bring some cash until you are certain.

- *Bring a comfortable shopping bag or small cart.* First time shoppers may want to bring a small backpack or shoulder bag that is comfortable to wear with heavier produce items. Having extra cloth bags may help.

- *Dress for the weather.* Wear good walking shoes and check the weather before leaving. Markets may be located in windy, sunny or exposed areas. Don't forget to tuck an umbrella in your car.

- *Plan your route.* Some items may need refrigeration, so plan ahead with coolers and ice packs, if food is stored in the car.

Simple Steps for the Farmers' Market

- *Tour first.* Take a walk around the market when you first arrive to see every product and compare quality and prices. Adjust your shopping list and mark any substitutions while touring the market.

- *Go with an open mind.* If you are unfamiliar with the growing season in your area, think of the farmers' market as an adventure in food. There are different varieties of the same foods, so the look, taste and smell may be different. Pay for a small sample before you buy.

- *Nature loves variety.* Unlike the grocery store which only stocks a standard size, shape and color of a food, nature is full of variety. There may be blemishes on the skin that is harmless but unfamiliar. Many imperfections come from nature rather than poor farming techniques or unsafe practices.

- *Specialty foods.* Farmers bring products that are not available at supermarkets: heirloom varieties, specialty cheeses, homemade pickles, sauces, etc. Each market has unique products of both cultivated and wild foods that are unique to your region.

- *Try new foods more than once.* Often, it takes many exposures of a new food before our palate may respond. Research shows that it takes 12 - 20 tastes before a new food may be appealing!

- *Involve children.* Children are more likely to try new foods when they are involved. Give children a small amount of change to spend or let them pick out the supper vegetable. Many markets have special events for children.

- *Ask questions – talk with the farmers!* Farmers welcome questions about their food, so don't hesitate to ask. They give samples so you can taste their produce – offer to pay if this happens.

- *Encourage sustainable methods.* Farmers take great pride in their products and are happy to explain their production. You can ask about pesticide or fertilizer use, organic farming methods, etc. They also consider your suggestions and explain their farming philosophy.

- *Show your appreciation.* Farmers make our local food supply secure and are a vital part of our communities – they appreciate our thanks.

Chapter 14:
Community Supported Agriculture (CSA)

If you are an adventurous eater, a Community Supported Agriculture Farm (CSA) membership is for you. A CSA is an agreement between farmers and consumers in the form of a membership, or "shares" of a farm. A farmer sells shares of the season to members and then delivers the product to the members on a regular schedule, usually at a central location convenient to the customers. Each week, opening the box is like a surprise birthday gift – you may not know what new item became ripe this week. Some CSA growers add nice touches like putting some edible flowers on top of the produce.

The CSA arrangement shares the benefits and risks of agricultural production. Members join before the start of the season so that the farmer has capital to invest in equipment, seeds and inputs to start the next growing season. From the beginning of the harvest season until weather conditions stop the growing season, the members get a box of produce each week. The farmer benefits with a secure customer base and the member enjoys high quality food each week. Both farmer and customer share the risk of food production due to effects of weather, pests and predators.

The duration of the membership may vary. For instance, membership may be for a full, half or quarter share. Each of these relate to quantity of food. The farmer will be able to tell you how much food is in each of these and how many people this would feed. One full share usually supplies enough produce for a family of two or four for one week. Half-shares or quarter-share are a portion of the full share amount. Farmers often offer working memberships so that you could donate a determined number of hours per week in exchange for the box of food.

If you are a cautious eater, you may want to share with friends or family so that you can each divide the box according to your tastes. Remember that it takes multiple exposures to a new food before our taste buds adjust. I have gone from not recognizing celeriac to tolerating small bites to looking forward to enjoying an entire bulb by myself.

CSA Advantages For the Consumer

- *Pay a fairer price.* A full-share price varies across the country from $13 to $47, with the average around $25 for 8 - 16 pounds of produce per week.

- *Save time.* Farmers have drop sites within the community where members pick up their boxes each week. You have all of your weekly produce shopping done in one stop.

- *Eat more variety.* The CSA box changes throughout the season and each box has five or more different foods. This variety is often not available to grocery store shoppers or may only be available in specialty stores.

- *Better tasting food.* Farmers are able to choose plants that have better taste rather than plants with qualities that must survive transportation over long distances, as in non-local produce. This results in better tasting varieties which are not possible in the grocery stores.

- *Learn about food and cooking.* A newsletter is sent with the box and the farmer describes the farm conditions of the week, lists the contents of the box and often provides recipes or other information about the food.

- *Know your farmer.* Volunteer workdays, involvement with the newsletter, or farm celebration tours are designed for you to become familiar with "your" farm. Children eat more produce if they are involved with their food production.

- *Increase rural-urban understanding.* Knowing each other helps form community. This mutual interest helps preserve family farms and increases our respect for food.

- *Multiply your investment.* Food that is spent locally circulates within your community. For each dollar you spend locally, $1.50 - $3.00 is generated.

CSA Advantages For the Farmer

- *Capital investment.* Farmers have money for the start-up costs of the season, equipment repairs and labor costs from planting and weeding, which membership fees will cover. Farmers plan their improvements with a secure membership base and income from year to year.

- *Connection to their customers.* Farmers have a secure customer base of members investing in his farm. This provides a volunteer base for developing newsletters, sharing recipes, volunteer work days and marketing.

- *Share the risk of farming.* With the natural flows of nature such as temperature fluctuations, pest loads or other seasonal changes, crop yield is more or less in any given year. Members are willing to accept more or less of a crop.

- *Efficient farming.* The farmer plans his planting based on the number of members, eliminating overproduction waste. Farmers also save on marketing costs.

- *Preservation of family farms and farmland.* CSA farming enables small to mid-sized farms to produce a livable wage for the farmers who otherwise cannot compete in the industrialized farm sector. The different crops needed for each box benefit the ecosystem, provide biodiversity, and preserve the soil.

Simple Steps to Join a CSA

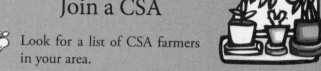

Look for a list of CSA farmers in your area.

Think about sharing a membership for the first year.

Visit the farm and see the production.

Be adventurous in trying new foods.

Involve your children.

Give feedback to your farmer, both positive and negative.

Be patient, adjust slowly to a new healthier eating.

Get to know other members and swap food from your box.

Celebrate! CSA is a winning combo for everyone.

Chapter 15:
Farm Stands &
Local Farms

As I drive across my home state, Wisconsin, in the summer, there are farm stands of all kinds. Near an intersection hosting a sign that attracts the motorists, is a self-serve stand, with a table, price sign and jar for money. Other stands are small buildings with shelves, counters and refrigerators. Farm stands are directly operated by the farmer on or near their property, usually with family members or staff assisting with sales.

Our neighborhood farm stand has one large permanent building with walk-in coolers, two refrigerators, counters and wagons of produce, shelves with value added products such as fruit butters, pickles and sauces, U-pick fields, and a greenhouse for bedding and garden plants. The farm stand sells products from their own and surrounding farms. Located right on the highway, the farm attracts many customers, including visitors and neighbors. The farm has many types of food and food processing available, from customers picking their own in the field, to choosing from the bins, to buying jars of preserves. Customers get a discounted price for every part of the process they are willing to do themselves.

Farm stands have several advantages for customers. You choose the amount and size of the product you need; get first-hand knowledge about your food, and save the costs of packaging. These stands usually offer an abundance of local varieties throughout the season. You can also negotiate a price for larger quantities. Frequent shopping acquaints you with the seasonal food calendar so you can plan menus around available food.

Farm stands may be located closer to you than any store or farmers' market, offering convenient shopping. The proximity of the stand to the fields where the food is grown helps the farmer provide freshly harvested food each day, so you have access to the freshest food possible. Because farmers are selling their own products, the amount and variety may be less than a farmers' market.

For any question you may have about the current harvest, upcoming produce or production methods, the farmer is usually available. Another delightful advantage of visiting local farms is that you get a glimpse of the farm operation. You can see and know whom you are supporting with your food dollars. Farmers are often happy to show customers around or discuss a particular farming method. Families learn to connect their food with a person and a place.

Farm stands help build community: You may find your neighbors at the stand, and catch up on community news when you stop. The farmer can provide a lot of information about the growing season and challenges of farming. Through these conversations, you hear how small farmers are faring in your community and the issues that concern the farming community.

Farmers benefit from a direct relationship to the customer. Through your conversations, the farmer knows the concerns of customers, specific foods to plant for next year, your level of knowledge about cooking and food preservation, and farming methods that concern you. Because supply and demand are right on the farm, the farmer harvests as needed each day, keeping the food in the field longer. The farmer saves transportation time and money, which helps lower food prices.

Simple Steps to Shop at a Farm Stand

- *Find local farm stands.* You may find these by driving through your neighborhood farmland or asking neighbors or community groups. Some communities publish a list of farms, including farm stands.

- *Note the hours the stand is open.* Small stands may be self-serve but if you want to ask questions, be sure that the farmer or an employee is available during the time you want to visit.

- *Bring cash in small bills and change.* Since farmers often do not have access to a nearby bank and are dealing with small purchases, it is best to have nearly the correct change.

- The convenience of the farm stand assures that you can *return for more produce.*

- *Buy what you are able to use and preserve.* Ask your farmer for different ways to cook and preserve the food, especially with new varieties that are unfamiliar to you.

- *Check for the abundance and availability of your favorite foods.* Buying at the height of the season when the fields are full is the best time to negotiate a price for larger quantities. Farmers appreciate pre-orders for large quantities.

- *Ask questions and give feedback*. Farmers enjoy talking about their products and appreciate hearing from customers, especially your favorite experience. Most farmers will listen and respond to requests from customers, if possible. If this is not possible, the farmer will tell you why.

- *Encourage family and friends to support their local farm stand*. Keeping agricultural knowledge alive in your community assures a supply of food in the future.

- *Find out about the issues challenging your local farmers and be a supporter*. Sustainable agriculture protects the land and water is beneficial for everyone.

Simple Steps for Visiting Your Local Farm

- *Confirm your visit with the farmer*, unless hours are posted.

- *Leave pets at home*. Many farms have animals such as dogs, cats, or poultry freely roaming the yard.

- *Keep a careful eye on your children* who may be unfamiliar about safety issues on a farm.

- *Wear sensible shoes* that could get dirty or muddy; you will be walking on uneven ground.

- *Follow paths* and keep gates or doors closed.

- *Be cautious* around livestock and other farm animals.

- *Only pick food if invited*. Remember the food is the farmer's livelihood.

- *If you are harvesting*, bring your own containers and wear protective clothing.

Chapter 16: Google & the Internet

Local food is easier to find thanks to the internet and the innovative folks who have compiled online lists of farmers, farm markets and restaurants. You can quickly search the internet to find local food and people supporting your farmers. There is much to learn about eating sustainably, supporting innovative farmers and improving community food systems. The following suggestions provide a skeletal framework for getting started – this is not a comprehensive list since the internet changes rapidly.

National websites such as Sustainable Table (www.sustainabletable.org) help educate consumers about local sustainable food and building community. Find another notable website for learning about eating locally at FoodRoutes Network (www.foodroutes.org), a nonprofit group that promotes local food through technical assistance and education. Their "Buy Fresh Buy Local" campaign has many state chapters.

Government websites provide information about programs, educational material or data. Search the United States Department of Agriculture (USDA) website (www.usda.gov) to learn more about food and nutrition programs, alternative farming systems and the national organic program, Know your Food, Know Your Farmer program, and many others. The Economic Research Service as part of the USDA reports affordability of the U.S. food system (www.ers.usda.gov).

Information about farming, specifically about sustainable agriculture and family farms is found easily on the web, starting with the following sites. The National Sustainable Agriculture Information Service at http://attra.ncat.org provides information and technical assistance about sustainable agriculture to farmers, ranchers and educators. National Family Farm Coalition (www.nffc.net), a nonprofit group, focuses on family farms and rural communities. FarmAid (www.farmaid.org) is a nonprofit orga-

nization that supports family farms with information and resources.

Other websites have extensive lists of farmers and farmers' markets near you. Two national guides to finding local food across the U.S. are the Eat Well Guide (www.eatwellguide.org) and Local Harvest (www.localharvest.org), which lists farms, farmers' markets, restaurants and more through their interactive maps. Slow Food USA (www.slowfoodusa.org) has local chapters in each state which frequently list restaurants that use local food.

Keep in mind that some farmers may chose not use the internet as a place to market their farm. Farming is an all-consuming job, leaving little time for maintaining a website or updating online information. However, farmers recognize effective marketing and may willingly list in a community brochure. These area guides may be available online.

Communities realize the importance of a local food economy and many community or regional groups are forming. Use "local food" and your state or city as key search terms. These groups are networks of information for all aspects of a local food system from farm to plate with valuable tools on their website.

See also: Resources chapter in this book, as well as the extensive local foods resources section at www.eatlocalsimplesteps.com.

Chapter 17: Co-ops & Natural Food Stores

I walked into a small co-op that had been recently renovated from an old gas station. As I entered, a tall, friendly man asked if I wanted a tour. Looking around, I smiled to myself thinking of the small space and imagined a quick five minutes. A full thirty minutes later, I knew more about the local farmers and producers in the area than I imagined possible. The tour guide, a store manager, knew the story of each farm in the area, the culinary aspects of the food and any unusual or quirky facts. This small store, Just Local Food, in Eau Claire, WI offered a snapshot of the whole local food scene.

Co-operatives are stores owned cooperatively by its members. They typically start as small buying clubs or a few families seeking to gain advantage of wholesale prices. Members can offer their labor or expertise. Often co-ops start in small spaces and grow with demand – they can grow in size to a membership list of hundreds or thousands. There is often a membership fee and/or vol-  unteer hours for discounted prices. Because co-ops are small, their needs may easily be met with local farmers. Co-ops are a great way for farmers to learn the particulars of selling to retail stores and to advertise their products. Co-ops may add shelf tags that indicate local or regional. Co-ops offer many foods in bulk so the prices are lower than comparable packaged foods but less waste is generated. With quick turnover, the products may also be fresher.

Locally owned natural food stores often have small sections dedicated to local fresh foods or locally processed foods. Like co-ops, their small inventory offer opportunities for small producers. Owners of natural food stores are interested in the health connection with food and are familiar outlets for customers looking for unprocessed and organic products. Because these stores offer specialty products, prices are competitive for suppliers and difficult-to-find products may be offered.

Both co-ops and natural food stores are interested in the needs of their customers and usually respond quickly to demand. If you are interested in specific local foods, educational programs such as nutrition or cooking classes, these stores may be willing to provide these or connect you with someone who can. These locally owned stores develop a network and dependence within the community.

Simple Steps:
Co-ops & Natural Food Stores

- Locate food co-ops and natural food stores in your area.

- Ask about the local food that is available. Tell the store manager about your interest and support of local foods.

- Ask the manager to offer a comparative price break on local products to support and encourage other customers to notice and buy local.

Chapter 18: Newspapers & Magazines

Communities celebrate local food in many ways; these may include harvest festivals, cultural and music festivals (combined with food), bake sales, county fairs, church picnics and other events. A special earmark of food festivals is their unique, local connections: if you live in Gilroy, California, you may go to the Gilroy Garlic Festival; to the Potato Feast Days if you live in Houlton, Maine; or to the Pasadena Strawberry Festival in Pasadena, Texas.

Local newspapers are one of the best ways to find out about your local food scene. There may be a weekly section dedicated to food, or a community events page dedicated to local happenings; restaurants may advertise seasonal specials or support of local farmers; and U-pick farmers alert us to the start of the season or gardening tips. Through your local newspaper, you find businesses that support your local food economy; issues that affect your food supply; and chefs dedicated to local food on their menus. A weekly publication often features goods wanted or sold. You may find used equipment for your kitchen or garden; garden inputs such as plants or compost for sale; dates for farmers' markets, or U-picks listed.

Edible Communities, Inc. is a publishing company that works with communities to develop regional magazines dedicated to local food environments. There are Edible magazines for cities such as *Edible Missoula* or *Edible Portland*, or regions such as *Edible Ohio Valley* or *Edible San Juan Mountains*. These magazines are beautifully illustrated with articles about your local food heroes – farmers, chefs, restaurateurs and food activists.

Edible features local processors such as a bakery, candy maker or winery. The articles and ads identify those interested in local foods. Often, we are unaware of the breadth of the local food movement in our own areas.

There are many other magazines dedicated to a local food area, many with the word "flavor" in their title. To find a magazine in your region, you can search electronically using key terms: (your city or region), plus "local food" or "local flavor."

If you visit any of the places you find through magazines or newspapers, tell the owner that you sourced their place through these outlets. People like to know that their listing is effective and your feedback is appreciated.

Simple Steps: Newspapers & Magazines

🍎 Browse through your newspaper, looking for local food related events: fairs, church dinners, gardening clubs, etc. Look in various sections of the newspaper.

🍎 Look for a weekly publication, often free, for local food opportunities, such as U-pick crops.

🍎 Search the library and internet for local food magazines, such as Edible Communities.

🍎 When traveling, notice local food news and bring home copies. Sharing ideas from other communities may spur activity in our own.

Chapter 19: Buying Clubs

Our local coffee roaster offers wholesale prices for large orders. A group of avid coffee drinkers, including my family, orders one large shipment per month – each family chooses five-pound bags of freshly roasted coffee. We swap smaller portions of different coffees and enjoy organic, Fair Trade, freshly roasted coffee for a budget price. Buying clubs such as this offer hefty savings. All you need is a network of people and a plan for ordering and delivery.

Producers and processors prefer to sell in large quantities since this saves time and money. You can take advantage of this by forming or joining a buying club. Our local food co-op started as a buying club, and grew into a general business. Ask your local food co-op, natural food store or farmer if there is an existing buying club that buys in bulk.

Buying clubs leverage more power for your money; they help you connect with local producers, and provide support for local eating.

Simple Steps to Form a Buying Club:

Decide on the common foods. This determines where to find your food. For instance, many groups celebrate Local Food week dedicated to one week of local eating. This group may want to keep accessing local foods throughout the year. Another group, 100 Mile Diet (http://100milediet.org), only purchases within 100 miles and limits the producers within this radius. Start with a potluck meeting to talk about your ideas and decide the organization.

Find a willing farmer, food producer or business and tap into an existing ordering or delivery system. Look for a producer  who can deliver a variety of foods or partner with other farmers to supply the group. You may also find an independent grocer, such as food co-op or natural food store, who makes the trip to the distribution center or has a delivery route. These farmers or owners may ask for a monthly fee to cover their time or fuel costs.

Determine the minimum order for the best price. This may be by volume or by price. A local grain miller may only sell in large sacks while our maple syrup farmer sells in various sizes and prices. Identify someone to organize the order, take turns coordinating the ordering, or rely on the farmer or storeowner. Clarify the procedures for payment.

Organize a plan for ordering and locate a drop spot for members to pick up their orders. There must be a central place for listing the food, either electronically or manually. The drop spot is usually informal, such as a garage, or formal such as a store. At pick-up time, you can celebrate your buying club community with a combination of food distribution and potluck social event.

Chapter 20: Other Places to Purchase Local Foods

Many communities have organized in innovative ways to support local farmers and make local food available. They often create local lists of available foods within the area, including growers' contact information, product descriptions and agricultural practices. Restaurants that support local food, farmers' market locations and community food festivals are often included. These local food listings require dedicated volunteers to locate farmers, gather the information and distribute around the local community. Most are distributed freely around the community.

Hospitals are one of the institutions that are reevaluating the food that they serve, changing to healthier food preparation, while recognizing the impact that health care has on communities in both influence and buying power.

Health Care Without Harm (www.noharm.org) is an international coalition group of health care facilities, health care professionals and communities that support practices to promote the health of people and the environment. Hospitals participating in the program take a pledge to support food systems that are ecologically, economically and socially responsible. Changes focus on increasing local food in the facilities, protecting biodiversity, reducing pesticide load and reducing waste. The health care facilities that honor this pledge work closely with communities within the local food system. You can check their online listing to see which facility has taken the pledge.

Similarly, the Physicians Committee for Responsible Medicine, which has launched the Healthy Food in Health Care Initiative, supports sustainable agriculture, reduces food waste and emphasizes nutritionally rich foods.

Often institutions do not have the time, equipment or labor to transform the farm fresh food into a quick serve product, such as peeled and chopped vegetables, but require processing by commercial facilities where food safety regulations are met.

A community kitchen or incubator kitchen offers facilities for either entrepreneurial food processing or nonprofit processing, with commercial kitchen equipment in a licensed kitchen facility. Small businesses or nonprofits share the equipment and facilities to process local food and have it available to the local community.

Community kitchens are gathering places for groups to gather around food, such as cooking classes, communal food preservation or community meals. You can find community kitchens in your area through an internet search, community college or extension office.

Simple Steps: Other Places to Purchase Local Foods

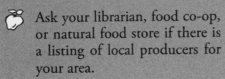 Ask your librarian, food co-op, or natural food store if there is a listing of local producers for your area.

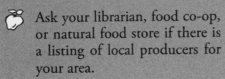 Ask your area hospitals to take the "Healthy Food in Healthcare Pledge".

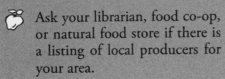 Ask the food service supervisor in the hospital cafeteria if local food is served. If not, encourage the hospital to consider this.

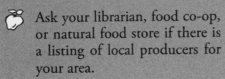 Search for a community kitchen near you and gather friends to preserve food in large batches or start local food potluck dinners.

Chapter 21: Restaurants

A few years ago, we hosted Odessa Piper, a chef famous for her dedicated use of local food in her Wisconsin restaurant, L'Etoile. At the informal potluck community gathering, I was struck by the conversation between Odessa and our local farmers as they excitedly talked about the specific varieties of greens, then other crops (I did not recognize half of the names), each characteristic relating to growing, cooking, and eating – a robust appreciation for food!

A good cook appreciates the flavors and aromas of freshly harvested food, speaking passionately about the best variety of eggplant or pear for a dish. Local food gives chefs a wider palate for creative cooking which is a compelling reason to include local items on menus. Seasonal menus keep customers intrigued and returning; unique combinations are possible with the diversity found on local farms.

Farmers appreciate chefs' ability to taste the finer qualities of their food, such as subtle flavors and textures. Chefs likewise are committed to helping keep food production and processes available in the region, as they are aware that foods derive their distinctive characteristics from the unique, specific environments of the land. Maple syrup tastes vary in different parts of the northern region; San Francisco wild yeast gives sourdough its unique flavor, and vintners know that local conditions influences wine flavors. Supporting a local food shed keeps this knowledge within the community and available to chefs.

The rise of fast food and globalization changed restaurants from local mom & pop diners featuring unique homemade foods into predictably common diners or strangely unique, gourmet eateries. These two extremes of sourcing food – from the same fast food chain supplier or global suppliers specializing in exotic species – led to food that is either lacking in taste or in familiarity. Meanwhile, the local farmer cannot compete for market space. With the resurgence in local foods, farmers are frequently partnering with chefs to provide fresh, familiar and flavorful food to both small diners and gourmet restaurants. Local food is back on the menu.

Check the menu. Independent, non-franchised restaurants, which have more flexibility and control over their menus, are more likely to source local. There may be a famous local food which is featured as a standard menu item, such as mac n' cheese made with a Vermont 10-year cheddar cheese. Daily or weekly specials give the chef an opportunity to use seasonal or less abundant supplies of local food. These unique foods are listed on the menu board or described by the wait staff. Friends and I stopped for breakfast in a small town and noticed the farm that supplied the eggs listed on the menu. When I asked the waiter about this, he told me the origin of every ingredient in the dish that I ordered, including when the food was delivered to the restaurant. That was service!

Ask about local. As in grocery stores, local food may be available but not advertised. Ask about local ingredients and where the food comes from. The wait staff will be the first available person but may not be as knowledgeable as the chef or owner. Some local food may have a specific season and therefore irregular appearance in the restaurant. In larger cities, chefs routinely shop the farmers' markets for their daily or weekly menu but may not make these changes on the printed menu – so ask.

Encourage local. As in grocery stores, owners depend on your business. If chefs and owners know your interest in local food, they are encouraged to seek local foods. You recognize the challenges with using local food, such as availability, cost, preparation time, delivery or cooking skill. Your encour-  agement may make a difference in whether a chef or owner sees value in using local food. If you know farmers eager to sell to local restaurants, be supportive of both restaurant and farmer. Sometimes this relationship takes time to build. Encourage friends and family to ask about local food where they eat.

Choose local menu items. You vote for a menu item each time you order! If local is on the menu, try the food and give feedback to the wait staff, chef and owner. Your satisfaction is the key to their success. The more adventurous you are as a customer, the more the chef plays with flavors and creates new dishes. Ask about any experimental dish from the chef, often an idea inspired by the farmers' market visit that morning.

Support local restaurants. Independent restaurants are able to respond quickly to customers. Often, there are guides to local restaurants in your community. Find the group that publishes these and ask that restaurants that are locally owned and use local food be designated. Supporting local has a domino effect in community and your dollars can double as it circulates. Choose these restaurants  when you eat out and ask the same of your friends and relatives. A group of chefs and supporters began The Chef's Collaborative (www.chefscollaborative.org) to educate and encourage the use of local foods in restaurants. This group is open to anyone who supports a biodiverse, sustainable, local food system.

Simple Steps to Encourage Local Food in Restaurants

- Check the menu for names of farms or farmers listed with menu items.

- Ask about local food on the menu.

- Speak with the chef or owner about local food being used.

- Encourage chefs and owners to use local food.

- Encourage restaurants to identify farmers and local food.

- Encourage your family and friends to eat locally at places that serve local food.

- Join The Chef's Collaborative and educate others in your community.

Chapter 22: Pick Your Own (U-Pick)

Discover some of best quality, freshest produce directly from the farm through Pick Your Own (PYO) or U-pick farms, where you hand-pick your own food. There are many advantages to picking your own. You can choose your size of produce and quantity and become familiar with different plants while enjoying a reduced price for harvesting your own – this makes it economical to pick for eating and preserving. My daughter remembers being in the field with me and picking strawberries. Her warmest memories are the laughter and chatter as we picked, cleaned and processed luscious fruit. Now grown, she is creating food memories with her own children.

Simple Steps to Prepare to Pick Produce

- *Call ahead.* People may have already picked the mature produce that day and you may have to wait a day or two for mature fruit. So call before leaving home.
- *Have cash ready.* Many U-pick farms accept debit and charge cards but smaller ones may not; call to verify or carry cash.
- *Bring your own containers.* Most U-picks have some containers available but will charge. Small, shallow containers are best for delicate fruit such as berries; half bushels are adequate without being heavy when full.
- *Wear sunscreen and a hat.*
- *Wear layers of clothes and closed-toed shoes.* A long sleeve shirt and long pants will protect you from any prickly bushes or insects.

- *Children are usually welcome*, but verify this with the farmer.
- *Pick in the morning.* It will be cooler which is better for the produce and comfortable for you.
- *Bring ice* for the produce if you will be out all day.
- *Bring your own shears,* if possible and necessary. Fruit such as grapes are picked by cutting the clusters. It is better for you and the plant to cut the small stem.
- *Pack a picnic.* Check the farm for information about shady picnic areas.
- *Consider carpooling.* Picking with others makes the time more enjoyable.
- *Plan on the time to clean and store your harvest when you return.*
- *Helpful websites for finding farms:* http://www.harvest4you.com; http://www.Pickyourown.org

Simple Steps to Pick Your Own

- *Check for ripeness before picking,* and purchase everything you pick.
- *Ask farmers to learn how to identify the best fruit* and ask for any special picking instructions.
- *Thoroughly pick a patch* or section to reduce waste in the field.
- *Use ladders for tree fruit and follow paths* for ground plants to avoid damaging plants.
- *Keep children safe.*
- *Respect the growers and their farm.* Do not throw produce or litter.
- *Buy enough produce for preservation.* Share with friends and family.

Chapter 23: Questions to Ask Farmers

A relationship with a farmer is not a typical supplier-customer relationship: We can do without many goods and services but we need to eat. Since most of us are ignorant about how to grow our own food, we are dependent on, and grateful to, the farmer. Each time one of my small garden crops, such as our recent tomato harvest, does not produce enough to last the year, our fail-safe is to go the farmer, whether that is via the fresh, frozen or canned grocery section or directly from the farmer. In the end, the farmers drive our food supply and know the most about their products.

A relationship with your local farmer may be the best food security you have. With less than one percent of our people listing farming as their primary occupation, you are fortunate to be able to meet, know and support a farmer. Having farmers near you is becoming increasingly valuable as soil, water and oil become expensive (and scarce), making long-distance growing and transporting more prohibitive. Food security for our fami-

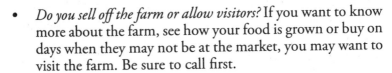

lies and communities involves growing the majority of our food as close as possible and assuring that we use sustainable practices to keep land in production for many generations.

Become a regular customer and supporter of farmers. Get to know them and their operations well enough to know both the opportunities and challenges of farming. Buy routinely from farmers and encourage friends and family to do the same. Learn about factors that affect farming such as weather, water, fuel prices, market availability, zoning, inheritance laws and commodity pricing, as well as food and price relationships. Establish a relationship with your farmer and inform him of your commitment to buying local.

First questions to ask farmers:

- *How long have you or your family been farming?* A heritage of family farming means extended caretaking of the land and the ability to see changes over time.

- *Where is the farm?* Not all markets have local farmers. Remember, the closer the farm, the more directly you support your local economy.

- *How large is the farm?* Supporting small to mid-size farmers keeps family farms as viable livelihoods.

- *What products are produced?* Ask about the diversity of the farm and specifics about products as you learn more about the seasons. A more diverse farm is better for the soil and the environment.

- *Do you sell off the farm or allow visitors?* If you want to know more about the farm, see how your food is grown or buy on days when they may not be at the market, you may want to visit the farm. Be sure to call first.

- *What would you recommend?* Farmers know the quality of their product better than anyone else and can describe unique features of a varietal, the peak of a season, or a new food in your area. Be open to the suggestions and adventures of food.

- *Ask for cooking and preparation tips* (especially with new or unfamiliar varieties). It is not easy to identify parts of an unfamiliar plant that need to be trimmed or anticipate the change in texture when a food is cooked – farmers provide this information.

- *When is the food harvested? What is the optimal storage time and technique?* Farmers are able to give you storage suggestions based on the fragility of the crop. The higher the water content and more fragile the cell walls, the faster a crop will deteriorate. Some foods are best at room temperature, require cold storage, or need refrigeration. Proper storing extends the quality of the food.

- *Is your farm certified organic or do you follow organic practices?* Don't just assume that all vendors at the farmers market are organic – many are not. Decreasing pesticides and herbicides safeguards the very foundations of our food system: soil, beneficial insects and water, as well as farm workers' health. Ask to see their certificate if it's not displayed.

Additional questions to ask farmers:

Here are a few more questions to ask the
farmers to support the sustainability of
a farm and increase the nutrient
value of your food (see more at
www.eatlocalsimplesteps.com):

- What organic matter is added
  back to the soil? Are crop residues
  left on? Is compost applied?

- If you farm organically but are not certified, what would
  you do to become certified? Farmers may not want the cost
  or may have different production methods.

- Does your farmer practice no tillage? The more the soil is
  tilled, the more damage to the soil structure, increased loss
  of organic matter and loss of soil organisms.

- Does the farmer practice low-
  carbon agriculture by limiting
  chemical inputs such as pesticides, herbicides, fertilizer?

- Does your farmer use crop rota-
  tions, cover crops and compost
  to manage pests and build nutrients?

Chapter 24:
Grow Your Own

You can grow the freshest, tastiest, and most satisfying food for pennies: Buy some seeds, plant in soil in a sunny location, water occasionally and wait for your bounty. It's that simple! Gardening is possible in any outdoor space, including porches or patios. If you have access to any land or container and sun, you can have a garden.

Why Garden?

Gardens are inexpensive. You may be surprised that seeds costs very little for the abundant yield. A carrot seed costs one penny or less; a nickel buys a bean seed, which yields more than a pound of beans. There is an initial investment in a small amount of equipment that is reused each year. Gardening is one of the least time consuming and most productive activities we can do. Therefore, your return on your investment is very high.

Gardens give you control over your food. You choose the food and decide the methods. Grocery stores can only offer a limited variety of produce while a garden gives you many choices. Browse through a seed catalog to get an idea of the possible abundance. As gardeners, our entire food supply is not solely dependent on food in the grocery stores. Our newfound knowledge helps us appreciate our local farmers, while understanding the natural world promotes good stewardship.

Gardens are healthy. Gardening activities help us maintain flexibility and strength. Gardening encourages us to know our environment and have a relationship with it, which is important for our health and well-being. People place value on familiar things. If you know the name of your plants or can describe the soil you have, you will see your world differently.

If you don't participate in a community garden, try to visit one. The array of vegetables and fruits planted and creativity in design can be very inspirational, and you'll come home with many new ideas. Growing your own food is easy with few simple steps and easy to find material.

What to grow

Temperature: The U.S. Department of Agriculture has been tracking the lowest temperatures since 1974. The U.S. is divided into eleven hardiness zones, reflecting the average minimal temperature in each zone. (See: http://www.usna.usda.gov/Hardzone). Zones are indicated on seed packets or seed description in catalogs, choose the plants indicated for your zone.

Plan: Pencil a design for your garden and start a notebook. Know what type of garden you prefer. A kitchen garden has cooking herbs, edible flowers and plants used immediately while a storage garden yields food for preservation such as tomatoes, onions and peppers for sauces.

Location: Plants need a well-drained, sunny spot (6-8 hours/ day). You need a convenient location to enjoy being in the garden and close to water.

Getting Help. Fellow gardeners have tips and quick tricks. Call your local state extension office to locate Master Gardeners or a local horticulture program. As you walk in your neighborhood, notice successful gardens or creative designs and stop to ask – fellow gardeners are eager to talk about their work.

Simple Steps for Gardening

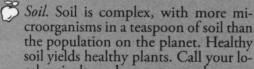

Soil. Soil is complex, with more microorganisms in a teaspoon of soil than the population on the planet. Healthy soil yields healthy plants. Call your local agriculture department to have your soil tested before you plant.

Seeds or plan. Start easy with high-yield plants or herbs – these are expensive in the store. Seeds are less expensive than plants, but often it is your skill and time that determine which to buy.

Pots. Any container that holds dirt can act as a pot for plants. Look around your house for various size containers that can hold plants, such as cans. Your imagination is your only limit.

Equipment. Minimum equipment includes garden gloves, shovel, trowel, hose, and a sharp knife or pruning shears.

Watering system. Collect free rainwater and use gravity feed whenever possible. Soaker hoses are more effective in watering plants.

Remember protection. Use a hat with a brim, sunglasses, sunscreen, and clothing that protects your skin.

Chapter 25: Foraging

Going wild! Foraging sounds like an exotic adventure, which it can be, but it may also be as simple as eating the dandelions from your lawn. Foraging is finding and eating edible, uncultivated food. You may be surprised at the abundance of food that surrounds you. Seattle residents, for example, pick 250 different plant species throughout the year; Maine residents are fortunate to forage for wild blueberries; and in Wisconsin where I live, fish from the state's numerous lakes is a foraged item. Search for "wild edibles" and "your state". Some of this food may be easily recognized, such as wild apple trees or roadside asparagus. Other food may take a keener eye and a guide, such as the many nonpoisonous mushrooms.

The abundance that is readily available is only limited by our knowledge of the plants around us. In the past, plant knowledge was kept vibrantly alive and passed through generations, along with locations for specific crops. We have added to the natural abundance as species from previous home gardens escaped into the wild, cross-bred and became part of our edible landscape. We may not realize the abundance before us. Recently, a relative from India was touring the garden, and grew

excited about a plant that is commonly eaten in India and highly prized. I was too embarrassed to tell her that I thought it was a weed and regularly put this in our compost bin, not realizing that it was a desirable vegetable.

Foraging includes an entire range of plants, including edible flowers, such as roses, violas, gladiolus and day lilies, to the more exotic passion flowers, hibiscus, and fuchsias. For generations, flowers have scented soups, syrups and candies, and been used in jams, puddings, sorbets and beverages. Naturally, they are beautiful edible garnishes.

If you are new to foraging follow these tips:

Where to find wild edibles

Anywhere plants grow is a potential harvest area. This includes not only large spaces such as woods and fields, but smaller areas such as sidewalk cracks or borders, empty city lots and roadside ditches.

Neighbors may have fruits, nuts or vegetables available. If you find unharvested plants or fruits, ask the neighbor for permission before picking. Often, people would rather have the food used than wasted. Rural land is private property. Public land is designated feet on either side of the road; be sure to ask the land owner before picking.

Identification

Read field guides. Identify the plants safe to eat by finding plant identification books in your local library or local horticultural specialist.

Find a mentor. Ask at your county extension office or senior citizen center for someone who knows the local landscape.

Attend a class. Check newspapers and libraries for announcements. Wildlife centers or university natural resource departments may offer classes on plant identification.

Know plant structure. If the entire plant is not safe to eat, some plant parts, such as flowers or bulbs, may be edible. Other plants need to be boiled or bitter parts removed before consumption. The age of the plant may also determine the taste. Some leaves become bitter with maturity; some wild apples become pleasing when stored rather than fresh. Use field guides or mentors for details.

Use caution

Check the laws. In some public spaces it is illegal to forage: call your local parks department for clarification. Foraging times may also be restricted to specific groups. Native American treaties may include foraging rights at specific times or areas.

Ask about pesticides and other chemicals. Your neighbor may be happy that you are picking the figs that drop over the fence line but may also regularly spray his yard with chemicals that you do not want to ingest. Parks use pesticides regularly and roadside crews may also use pesticides, or there may be pollutants from passing vehicles.

Start small. If you are new to foraging, take small amounts and forage often. Wild foods may have higher mineral contents and bolder flavors.

Be considerate. Foragers always leave some behind. There are other foragers, or the plant needs to mature to continue the reproductive cycle.

Children need attention. Be sure children check with an adult before ingesting any plant. Passing the knowledge is important for our children, but be confident that your child is identifying plants correctly before foraging on her own.

Simple Steps for Foraging

🍎 *Bring your field guide* or other notes for safe collecting.

🍎 *Bring a knife or scissors* since some foraging requires snipping or cutting rather than snapping.

🍎 *Have a gathering bucket,* basket or bag so you keep the food clean and bruise-free.

🍎 *Dress appropriately.* Foraging berries requires long sleeves and gloves to protect against the brambles.

🍎 *Many leaves and shoots are eaten raw in salads or added as a fresh garnish to a cooked dish.* Chopped chive stems or small purple chive flowers add a dash of color – both have a mild, onion flavor.

🍎 *Petals and seeds can be used as flavoring agents.* Syrups, jams, beverages, desserts can all be flavored. Adding rose petals to a small jar of sugar adds a unique flavor and pleasing scent.

🍎 *Soups and stews are favorite dishes for foraged foods.*

🍎 *Experiment with dried plants.* The calyx of the hibiscus, for instance, is dried and used later in a beverage. Dried lily buds are used in soups and stews. Rosemary and other herbs are used in cooking throughout the year. Fruit can be dehydrated.

Section III
Saving Money with Local Foods

Chapter 26:
Saving Money with Local Foods

Although food is a necessary daily expense, you can eat joyfully and healthfully on a small budget, using local food as a primary source for your meals.

Local, fresh food provides a beneficial, cost-effective alternative to the "cheap food" of the industrialized food system. At most farmers' markets, for example, the produce you buy is the highest quality since the farmer harvests close to market time. This food has bold, ripe flavor and color, unlike grocery store produce that is picked unripe and shipped long distances, then stored in a warehouse. Spoilage is also less with freshly harvested food.

High cost of cheap food

"Cheap food" is a myth, because food that nourishes deserves a fair price. "Cheap food" comes from government-subsidized crops such as wheat and corn. Government payment increases production of these crops – this drops the market price and the resulting low price enables food processors to have low cost ingredients. The profit of wheat and corn for food companies results from the transformation of inexpensive raw products into a variety of processed food products sold to consumers as convenience items available in the center aisles of grocery stores.

These food products with similar ingredients, artificial flavors and additives are the bulk of consumers' current purchases in the U.S. As a taxpayer, you are paying the agriculture subsidy and again paying for the processing, packaging, marketing and distribution of food products. The true cost of food is hidden while the myth of cheap food persists. Instead of consuming complex nutrient-rich foods with abundant vitamins, minerals, and phytochemicals, the food industry uses components of food, stripped of nutritional value. There is often little real food left in these products.

Another hidden cost of the cheap food is the escalating health costs of this diet. These poor diets lead to the development of obesity and chronic diseases such as heart disease, diabetes and certain cancers. Increased sick days and higher medical bills increase the cost of a poor diet. Transitioning to a nutrient-rich diet saves you money now and in the future. A quick path for health is as simple as a farm-fresh bunch of spinach or basket of raspberries.

The food industry uses marketing techniques to influence our purchases. One such effective technique is to convince us that we have hectic lifestyles with little time and that we want the food industry to do food preparation for us. Each packaging step adds cost to the consumer and uses un-

necessary resources. For example, the popular box of macaroni and cheese is perceived as inexpensive but you also need milk and butter. Essentially, you are buying pasta with a high sodium flavor packet. The same amount of pasta is less expensive and you control the ingredients.

Ready to eat salads, microwaveable meals, and vegetables already trimmed are marketing strategies that support convenience but cost consumers. You pay for the labor, the excess packaging and the preservatives added for freshness. Buying whole fruits and vegetables requires washing and some trimming but whole food stays fresher longer, is less expensive and generates little waste.

Food industry dependence

Farmers lose money when you purchase packaged and processed foods, receiving just nineteen cents for every food dollar you spend. Each time a food is processed, nutrients are lost and costs added. Buying directly from the farmer saves you money, increases the farmer's income, and circulates money in your community.

Our dependence on processed food results in less cooking from scratch. Because we do not cook, we do not shop for raw, unprocessed products and lose our ability to distinguish between whole foods, such as the best apple variety for applesauce or the best potato variety for mashing. We have less food and cooking knowledge being passed down to succeeding generations.

When you spend the effort to break out of dependence on supermarket convenience food shopping, replacing it or supplementing it with local food, your efforts will produce a lifetime of tasty meals; provide life skills that your children need; preserve your family food heritage; and assure that you have a future food supply. Investing in a sustainable local food supply is cost effective, enjoyable and secure!

Chapter 27: Planning

Using local foods requires planning but saves money. Purchasing foods at the farmers' market, for example, costs less than grocery store food shipped from long distances, because you cut out the middlemen by buying direct from the grower.

Inventory/awareness. Scrutinize your current food purchases. Do a review of your food budget and make a plan to get started by knowing your food staples and your food budget. Be vigilant in buying good quality foods within your budget.

Write a grocery list. Inventory your current food purchases by making a list of all foods in your house – this helps you distinguish between essential and discretionary ingredients and helps prioritize your food purchasing habits. Itemize the list as follows: staples in your cabinets, refrigerator and freezer; discretionary foods; and occasional items you use for food preparation. Staples are those foods that you use daily or weekly; these are the core of your eating and are kept in stock. As an example, pasta, rice or cereal may be regularly eaten or canned tomato products used routinely. Discretionary foods are those foods you purchase that are not necessary to your health but add interest and flavor or other value to your diet. While snack and dessert products are obvious discretionary purchases, there are others such as olives or pickled foods. Occasional items are products purchased for special occasions or infrequent use. I have spices, different mustards and flavored oils in my kitchen that I use less frequently.

Next, examine your list; underline the packaged foods and place an asterick next to the prepared foods. As an example, pasta or rice is packaged while the convenience products of frozen pasta

or rice based dinners or boxed pasta dinners are prepared. Some minimal amount of packaging and processing is necessary for some foods. The purpose is to identify those products with minimal packaging and preparation steps and determine how much of the processing is desirable within your budget. You may have fresh potatoes, frozen hashbrowns, frozen dinners with potatoes or potato chips, for example; each step reflects increased processing. Minimally processed and packaged foods are the best value for your dollar: With processed and packaged foods, you pay for every additional convenience while sacrificing nutrients. Review your list and identify which foods are absolutely necessary.

Focus on value. Become aware of non-nutritious food products in your diet and gradually eliminate them; eat food, not food products. Reduce or eliminate expensive snack foods and drinks that offer fat or sugar and little else, and replace with popcorn, or a handful of nuts, fruits and vegetables. Substitute whole foods, as close to their natural state and as close to harvest as possible, for the convenience foods you now buy; these provide maximum nutritional value, while seasonal foods assure variety. Local, whole foods are also less expensive, as you get more food for your money. An organic carrot or apple from the farmers' market may cost more, but you avoid the pesticides that come with a super-market variety – and it tastes better because it's fresher.

Purchase inexpensive foods. Use expensive ingredients sparingly. Animal foods are generally more expensive than plant foods, so consider limiting meat meals – this is an easy way to cut back on calories and expenses. Designate one meatless day per week to get started. Other days, emphasize the flavor of meat but reduce the quantity by using it in stir-fries and casseroles. You can afford better meats that are organic or pasture-raised if you reduce the quantity.

Portions. Gradually, we have supersized our meals and snacks. Concentrate on the variety and flavor of a nutrient rich diet rather than volume for optimal health. The USDA-sponsored website at www.myplate.gov is a great resource for finding recommended portions for every age. A quick look at your plate will help you plan a nutrient-rich meal with three-quarters of the plate filled with vegetables, whole grains, beans and fruits. A plant-based diet saves you the most money since the production costs are less and plant-based foods give you the most nutrients with the greatest health benefits.

Plan seasonally. Often recipes rely on our global market and include imported or out-of-season ingredients. Seasonal charts can help you plan meals by alerting you to the week or month when different ingredients are available at your farmers' market or produce section. Call or talk to your local farmers' market manager or independent bookstore owner about cookbooks featuring seasonal foods in your area. These cookbooks feature recipes that rotate by the season with the majority of ingredients available from farmers in your locale. You also get hints on making your favorite recipes more local.

Purchase large quantities in peak season. Purchase larger, bulk quantities directly from local farmers or processors when the crops are in full season to save money. The fresher the food, the longer it lasts, which is a better investment for your money. By purchasing in large quantities, you'll also pay less per serving.

Farmers' markets reflect the local growing season so you will notice small changes each week as you shop at the market. With each crop, the first of the season comes to the market in small quantities and is more expensive. As the season progresses, the crop is more abundant and the prices may drop. When a fruit or vegetable is in peak season, farmers often offer better prices for larger quantities (quarts or bushels) – this is a good bargain if you have the capacity for freezing, drying or canning. Remember that the initial investment will save money later. Think about a plan for a year, rather than a week or month.

Store, freeze or dry extra fruit and vegetables. Peak-season purchases at the market translate into abundance in your kitchen. Find ways to preserve this rich harvest: Fresh food may last longer in your crisper, or cool dark closet, for example. Enjoy the sight, smells and tastes of the peak-season market and know that you can return again and again.

You can use many tomatoes throughout the year and stretch the tomato supply from one season to the next by freezing whole tomatoes in a bag to pop into soups and stews; drying tomatoes to add to sauces and casseroles; and canning pasta sauce and salsa along with whole tomatoes. Sundried tomatoes seem exotic and high-priced in the stores but are inexpensive and easy to dry when you purchase peak-season tomatoes in the market and put a pan of cut tomatoes on your car dashboard for quick drying. Think about how you can save money with purchases by storing dried or frozen products for out-of-season eating.

Divide large purchases, such as bushels, with neighbors. Freeze or can the extras. My drive to our local cheese factory, for instance, saves money on both cheese and butter. Both keep well and I can stock up for the month. I also let friends know about my shopping trip and we take turns going to the cheese factory.

Variety. Purchase a variety of foods so that when you go home you have many options for cooking and eating. Weekly snacks and lunches are interesting when we have a variety of washed and trimmed raw foods ready to eat. Our palates are easily satisfied with a variety of flavors and textures.

Shop Frequently. Shop only for the amount of food that you know you will be able to use in the next week or are willing to preserve for later use. (See Chapter 31, "Food Preservation"). Food that eventually spoils in the back of your refrigerator or cabinet is wasted money. There is less spoilage and you are eating foods that are fresher and healthier. Small farm stands are dotted within a city, offering a convenient stop on your way home.

Experiment. Buy familiar food but experiment each week. You will expand your food choices without stretching your budget if you try a new food each week. Remember that it takes a dozen exposures to a new food before you or your children may like it.

Simple Steps for Planning a Food Budget

🍎 Using local foods can save significant money in your food budget.

🍎 Know essential daily or weekly foods. Choose these based on value (taste, environment, ethics, etc.) and health.

🍎 Scrutinize packaged and prepared foods. Small efforts, such as washing and cutting produce or combining basic ingredients, save big money.

🍎 Eliminate waste. If you buy it, eat it.

🍎 Learn to cook and eat seasonally.

🍎 Limit expensive foods and large portions.

🍎 Purchase during peak season for the best price.

🍎 Consider large purchases to save more money. Preserve for later use or split with friends or family.

Chapter 28:
Your Food Budget

Saving money begins with an awareness of your current food purchasing habits. You will find easy and inexpensive changes to increase your food value and support your personal beliefs with a few simple steps.

Getting started

Begin with recording your food purchases. For one week, each person in the household records all food and beverages, including water, that is purchased and consumed outside the home. Combine the individual lists onto a master food list and total the money spent. This tally represents food eaten away from home.

Next, record grocery purchases for the same week; note where you shop and keep your receipts to record the information in the price book described below. From this quick look, you can determine the amount you typically spend on food and stores you frequent. Lastly, add any bartered, traded or received food. For instance, if your family has a garden and regularly preserves food, the cost of your yearly food will be lower, with an initial investment during the gardening season. Just note what stored food you used this week.

Food allowance

Combine the totals of grocery purchases and food eaten away from home; multiply this amount by four to estimate your total monthly food expense. Use the following formula to determine the percentage of money you spend on food: (total dollars spent on monthly food ÷  total monthly income) x 100 = percent of income spent on food per month. This represents how much money you spend on food and is the starting point for determining your food budget. Americans spend an average of nine percent of their income on food purchases, which is the lowest anywhere in the world, reflecting our subsidized food system. To determine your food budget, recalculate the percentage of your income for food, if necessary. Generally, a minimum of eleven percent of your net income is necessary for healthy frugal food budgets.

Next, review your food purchases to determine if these are aligned with your goals for your lifestyle, health, and family. Do your food choices reflect your family values, support optimal health, invest in your local community, or educate your children? Given your goals, identify the food purchases that are supportive and discuss alternatives to the other foods on your list. This reflection helps prioritize your time and direct your purchasing power. The best value is not the least expensive, but food that provides the most return for your money and is aligned with your values.

The greatest return for your food dollar is nutrient-rich foods, such as foods low in added fats and sugars, whole foods, or minimally processed foods. Review your food list and circle nutrient-rich foods. These foods represent high value for your dollar and are mainstays in your budget. Check your list of foods for complete nutrition so each family member is eating a variety of foods from each food group. Consider the foods in your list that provide calories or convenience but little else – usually the longer the ingredient list, the less nutritious the food. Try to eliminate or reduce these items. A plant-based diet is economical and healthy; plan 60% of your budget for grains, fruits and vegetables and 30% foods high in protein to gain best health for the dollar.

Most Americans eat less than the recommended amounts for fruits and vegetables, often because they erroneously think they are too expensive and may not recognize their contribution to saving health dollars. My friends are surprised that the farmers' market has the lowest price for fruits and vegetables – this is true in many other communities as well. Check your assumptions about price by developing a price book.

Price book

Frugal shoppers have a tool called a price book which is a notebook of food purchases and prices – it helps you compare the price of foods from different sources. The first row is the titles of each column. In this title row, add "food" in the top of the first column;  follow across the row with the name of each place where you purchase groceries including the bakery, farmers' market, farm stands, and various grocery or convenience stores.

Return to the first column, labeled "food" and move down the column by adding each food that you purchased; it is best to categorize this by location in the store. For instance, list produce together, dairy products in another section, etc. You should have one complete list of all the foods purchased in the first column. This is the basic price book which lists the food and the places you obtain the food. As you visit each place, you add the price per quantity for each food purchased and compare prices.

This provides a running tally of items and prices at the places you shop. Be sure that you are comparing the same amount for the price. Fruit may be sold individually at the farmers' market but sold in bags in the grocery store. If you are buying organic produce from the farmer, compare the same organic food in the grocery store. Initially, the price book will take time, but once established, you will know where to shop to get the best value for your food dollar.

Simple Steps: Your Food Budget

- Record all food and money spent for one week, multiply by four to estimate your current monthly food expenditures.

- Identify foods that align with your values and goals.

- Determine the amount of money allotted for food each week.

- Complete the price book.

Chapter 29: Saving Money with Farmers

Farmers are interested in selling all that they grow, realizing that their products are perishable or require processing and storage. Since small to mid-size farmers have flexibility to work with consumers and small groups of people, they can be more responsive to your needs. Developing a relationship with farmers provides advantages for both you and the farmer.

Become familiar with food that the farmer produces and understand the growing seasons. Local food provides a wider variety than grocery stores so anticipate returning often to your favorite farmers' market or to a grocer who works with farmers. Expect to pay more for produce just as the season starts or when unusual practices are required such as extended season techniques.

Peak-season purchases. At the height of the season, produce is at its peak and abundant and there is urgency in getting the foods from the fields to the tables or freezers to retain maximum flavor and freshness. Save money by purchasing larger quantities

at the height of the season, such as tomatoes, peppers or apples by the bushel, or strawberries and raspberries by the flat. Buying in larger quantities is a better value for the consumer, especially if you can share this abundance with others or have the capacity to preserve the excess.

Cherish diversity. The standardization of products in the grocery store has misled customers into believing that nature produces food in uniform shapes and sizes. Perfect food costs more since nature produces fruits and vegetables with slight variations in contour and size. Local farmers often market produce that is larger or smaller than expected for a lesser price than larger or perfectly shaped produce. Our local farmer sells table carrots or cut-and-peel carrots that reflect differences in shape or size and are priced accordingly. Recognize blemishes on produce that are only surface scars and do not compromise quality – your farmer can explain the scabs or scars you see. Don't discard high quality food for a small scar.

U-pick. Save more money by harvesting the produce yourself when farmers offer U-pick days or gleaning days. Farmers recognize the value of time, money and labor and pass the savings to you when you provide these. U-pick farms open the farm for customers to pick their own, often using their own containers. The U-pick chapter in this book includes explanations and suggestions. Gleaning is opening the fields for picking after a mechanical harvesting has taken place. Consider inviting a group of family or friends to the farm to make the event a social outing.

Join a CSA. Join a Community Supported Agriculture (CSA) farm where you buy a subscription to a farm and receive a share routinely during the harvest season. A CSA share is less expensive than the equivalent food from the store, is higher quality, and provides more variety. CSA farmers usually offer U-pick days on the farm or discounts for working members – both offer further savings. There may also be a membership discount for low-income members.

Form a buying club. Another option is to form a buying club with friends and family and negotiate ordering from a farmer on a regular basis. This is more informal than a CSA but provides the farmer with a dedicated, pre-sold market. The farmer sends out a list of available foods that customers can order prior to delivery day. Since the farmer has a pre-sold product that she can deliver to a large number of people, there is usually a discounted price. In both a CSA and buying club, a central location saves traveling time for the farmer and provides the convenience of a central distribution point for the customers. See chapter 14, "CSAs," for more information.

Purchase in bulk. Farmers enjoy selling bulk and preordered items. Be sure to ask the farmer for any products which he would like to sell for a good price; there may be some new varieties for which he would like to build a market  and want to encourage customers to try these. Our area farmers offer bulk orders of a variety of foods that can be stored throughout the winter, such as varieties of potatoes, onions, squashes, carrots, celeriac, pumpkins and garlic. Many times unfamiliar new varieties end up being our family favorites.

Try new foods. Farmers are interested in developing a strong customer base either directly or through chefs and grocery store managers. Take advantage of this by fostering an interest in new foods and a willingness to trust the farmer when new varieties are offered. Farmers or grocers often give samples of foods and suggestions for preparations or pairing with other foods. They also give tips for handling and storage so you can get the benefit of the food while reducing waste. Ask farmers to identify a food; ask whether it is eaten raw and/or cooked; how perishable it may be, and different recipe suggestions. Make an effort to try at least one new food when you go to the market, so you get to know all the bounty in your area. If you often have different cultural foods in your area and are unfamiliar with how to choose the best ones or identify edible parts, you can rely on farmers to provide the basic information.

Reduce waste. A bargain from the farmer fails if you do not use the food, so reducing waste in your own house is paramount to saving money. Whole foods last longer since vegetables and fruits usually come with a protective skin or peel. The more exposed and increased the surface area, the faster deterioration occurs. Some foods keep longer if they are cleaned just

before cooking; some need to be kept at room temperature, while others need cool storage or refrigeration. Learn the art of storage and preparation by looking for information sheets from farm stands and markets; information booths sponsored by organizations or farm market management at the farmers' market; or the many cookbooks that feature local, seasonal cooking.

When preparing food, minimally trim ends or peels to minimize waste – if you buy organic foods you can scrub the peel and eat without removing it. Keep leaves or scraps in a bag in your refrigerator and make

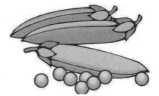

soup stock every few days. Maximize your food dollars by reducing waste through minimal trimming, making stock, and composting plant remains. Find more tips for saving money by preserving your own food at the height of the season in the Food Preservation chapter.

Simple Steps: Saving Money with Farmers

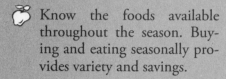 Know the foods available throughout the season. Buying and eating seasonally provides variety and savings.

Buy during the peak of the season for best prices.

Expect imperfect looking produce. Differences in size and shape are natural, you pay more for cosmetic perfection.

Harvest your own at Upick farms.

Join a Community Supported Agriculture (CSA) farm or buying club.

Build a relationship with your farmer.

Know how to store and prepare the food.

Be willing to try new varieties. New varieties may add interesting flavors or textures. Varieties may also be less expensive or have extended storage life.

Chapter 30: Farmers' Market Money Saving Tips

Each market has its own personality with its own unique food and features. The more familiar you are with the markets in your area, the more money you save as you anticipate the foods, know the prices and bargain with the farmers for the best deals. Economical shopping is based on your relationship with the farmers to know their techniques and learn their specialty crops. While many farmers in our area grow similar vegetables, we have one farmer who specializes in different garlic varieties, and another with many potato varieties. On a recent visit to the Santa Fe market, a farmer was selling a chili variety that has been grown by their family for four generations. Becoming a regular shopper at the market will help you recognize unique foods, best prices and highest quality.

Shop frequently and buy only what you can use in the next week, or are willing to preserve for later use. Farmers' market produce is harvested close to market time and while it will last longer than food transported over thousands of miles, peak flavor diminishes with time. Prevent spoilage and waste with smaller purchases. You'll need smaller amounts of market foods when cooking because fresh food is more flavorful!

Explore many farmers' markets. Because farmers adapt to customers' food choices, farmers' markets differ, often based on cultural preferences or income level. You can take advantage of this versatility by learning the times and locations of various markets in your area. Learn additional tips by listening to how local customers choose produce and describe preparation.

Menu planning for savings. The start of the market will have the most variety, which is why chefs shop early to have the most options. Touring the early market helps you become familiar with the different products, enabling you to plan for your meals with the most choices. It is best to have general menus planned and allow for flexibility of ingredients as you shop the market. The more familiar you become with the seasonal flow of food, the more you anticipate changes within your menu. In our area, the spring menu focuses on leafy greens, radishes, small turnips, asparagus and strawberries. You save money when you plan menus around the abundant products of the season, rather than come to the market looking for a specific ingredient that may not be in season.

Learn the pricing structure. Farmers ask for a fair price for their labor and specific product. Ask farmers about their prices so you understand the requirements of different production methods or characteristics of a product. Some foods require more labor, may be difficult to forage, or are only grown infrequently.

Production methods, such as organic farming, require more attention to soil health without chemical inputs to produce healthy plants. These inputs require more labor and thus cost more for the customer. Decreasing pesticide loads for family members who may be more vulnerable to health issues – such as the children and elderly, people with a history of cancer, or pregnant women – may be worth the extra price for organics. Learning about the pricing structures helps you evaluate food choices.

End of the day bargains. The end of the market may have the best prices as farmers would rather sell than return with food. Be prepared to buy larger quantities at the end of the market day for the best savings; if quantities are too large for your household, try sharing the costs with friends and family.

Avoid the temptation to monoshop. Buy more variety of foods rather than a large quantity of fewer foods; as the week progresses, you will have many ingredients for your meals and have a variety of flavors and nutrients. Many foods can be washed and trimmed for your work-week lunches. Having a small variety of raw foods will make the rest of your week's snacks more interesting. These same raw foods can be added to stir-fry and casseroles later in the week to change flavors. Quick meals are versatile and interesting with variety.

Take advantage of peak season: Farmers' markets reflect the local growing season so you will notice small changes each week as you shop at the market. Unlike the grocery store, where you see an arrival of a seasonal crop in large quantities, the first of the season comes to the market in small quantities. Like heralding the new babies, the first of the season blueberry or turnip is a celebrated event. These first showings may be slightly more expensive because they are in short supply and high demand.

As the season progresses and the fruit or vegetables are more abundant, however, the prices usually drop as more farmers have these available and want the quantity in their fields to move into customers' baskets. This peak season is the time to purchase larger quantities (quarts or bushels) if  you have the capacity for freezing or canning. Also, prime season is the time when fruits are sweetest! As you become more familiar with the peak season for different foods, you will be able to distribute your food budget. Each fall, I buy and roast extra corn for freezing and eating throughout the winter. The price is lower than frozen corn in the store and the taste is fresher.

Take advantage of the friendly (and flexible) farmers. The more often you shop and the more conversations that you have with farmers, the more familiar they are with your preferences and may be willing to grow what you need and want. You build trust with the farmer. I recently asked a farmer about lemongrass, which he did not have in his stand that day, but was happy to bring a few bunches from his garden the next day. Farmers may grow and sell at various markets and adjust their products based on the demands of each market. Unlike the supermarkets, small farms and farmers have this diversity, friendliness and flexibility. Be sure to see chapter 23 about questions to ask your farmer.

Get involved. Farmers' markets often depend on volunteers. Promoting and helping the farmers' market strengthens your local economy, enables farmers to stay in business, and keeps your food local and fresh – all of which guarantees a secure food source for you and your family. This also builds  community relationships as you get to know the person who grows your food and the farmer gets to know your family.

Simple Steps: Saving Money at Farmers' Markets

🐚 Shop frequently. For best freshness and keeping quality, shop often.

🐚 Shop for variety. To maximize the flavors, textures, prices and nutritional benefits, choose a variety of foods.

🐚 Find a variety of farmers' markets. Dynamic relationships between farmers and customers bring foods that are unique to neighborhood ethnic markets.

🐚 Find the best prices. End of the day, height of the season and bulk buying will save you money.

🐚 Know a farmer. Farmers share knowledge and cooking tips to help you make better choices.

🐚 Volunteer in the market. A strong market helps everyone in your community so be involved.

Chapter 31: Food Preservation

Drying

Drying is the oldest food preservation technique. You do not need special equipment or much time – just days when the sun is strong and the air is dry. Happily, the height of the season usually coincides with these types of days. Alternatively, you need a warm dry place in your house where you can suspend food while it dries. If this is not naturally available, there are dehydrators that can provide dry circulating heat.

The idea behind drying is to provide enough air circulation around the food so that the outside can begin to dry without any bacterial growth and the inside will dry fast enough to prevent any breakdown of the food and spoilage. My first and easiest attempts at drying were to hang bunches of herbs upside down to dry. The leaves dry fast since they are small with so much surface area that evaporation happens quickly. Considering the price of dried herbs, this was a quick, inexpensive way to get the herbs I needed for winter cooking for a small fraction of the bottled herb price. Herbs sitting in a jar in a cabinet year after year lose their potency. These herbs had a better color and flavor because they were freshly dried. Next, I strung the ends of chili peppers together and hung those from a nail on the kitchen wall. They looked beautiful and were accessible all winter long for adding to soups and sauces.

Foods with higher moisture, like tomatoes, figs, peaches, etc., need slightly more attention. These can be placed on racks, such as cooling racks for baking or those that come with the dehydrator. You can place in a box with a screen on top to keep away any insects and place in the sun or on the dash of your car during a hot afternoon. This may take a few days. Remember to bring the food inside during the evenings. You can also place on racks or trays in your oven at a low temperature for a few hours.

Drying tips

- Chose ripe fruit or vegetables that are firm but healthy.

- Wash the outside of the produce. Cut away any bruised spots.

- If large, slice into thinner sections. Remember produce with higher water content, like tomatoes, will shrink considerably.

- Suspend with string or place on racks.

- Dry in oven, dehydrator or directly in the sun (cover with screen to prevent from insects).

- Produce should be dry, slightly flexible (leathery) but not crisp.

- Store in bags in a dark cabinet or freezer.

Root Cellaring

If you live in a cooler climate and have unheated spaces, root cellars offer convenient, inexpensive produce storage. Root cellars require the opposite conditions of drying – moist air in a cold place. The late fall crops that are common in the northern states are  perfect for root cellars. Apples, pears, root crops such as carrots, turnips, parsnips, potatoes, etc., and hard skinned squash, are common candidates for root cellars. Think of the foods that keep well in the back of your refrigerator or cool pantry shelf. It is a treat to have a fresh carrot from a garden or bin in the middle of a snowy evening.

The simplest root cellar is to keep your produce in the ground, covered with enough mulch to prevent freezing. You can dig up the vegetables as you need them. Next, look for unheated space which may be a closed area in your outside buildings, an unheated closet or room in the basement or upstairs, or a hole in the ground. By opening or closing a window, you can control temperatures. Pans of water can control humidity. Various containers such as garbage cans, plastic bins, insulated coolers, and baskets can be used.

Root cellared produce requires temperatures just above freezing, 32° to 40°F and about 80% humidity. If you cannot keep a cold, humid space, an unheated room will extend the storage of many crops. Conditions for different vegetables and fruits vary so check out a food preservation book from your local library for more information.

Some produce needs to be separated. Fruits release ethylene gas which will sprout of some vegetables. Cabbage and turnips release odors that can be absorbed by other produce. There may be some varieties of produce that store better than others. Ask your  farmer about these. There are some varieties of apples which taste better after being stored and are a special treat.

Canning

I have a secure feeling as winter approaches when I open my pantry and see rows and rows of canned sauces, jellies, fruits and vegetables from our garden and farm market. Canning is a part of the garden ritual when the produce is stacked high on the counters. We do not have freezer space for all that we keep and some foods taste best when canned. It is easy to open a can of tomato sauce or soup when we want a fast meal.

Canning requires an initial investment in jars, bands, lids, a device for lifting jars out of hot water, and a canning pot or pressure canner. Often, canning pots can be found at rummage sales and second-hand stores. Jars may also be found in these places, but be sure to check that the rim does not have any chips or cracks. Grocery stores sell the lids and bands. Lids should be new each time but all other equipment can be reused.

Canning preserves food by adding hot food into jars and heating both jar and food until all pathogens are killed. High acid foods are canned in boiling water baths. These are large pans that have a rack on the bottom where you place the jars. Fill the pan with water above the jars so that jars are immersed completely in the water.

Low acid foods, such as carrots, beans and corn, need to be processed in a pressure canner. Because you heat the food first, there are some foods which are best to freeze rather than can, such as berries or night shade vegetables (eggplant, cabbage, and broccoli). Pressure canners use less water, since you only need a few inches of water to produce the steam necessary to can. The pressure canner has a gauge which helps you monitor the pressure.

It is very important that canning be done safely to avoid any food contamination, so check with your county extension agent for published guides for canning and the latest information about food safety. These are easily available online on extension websites and can be downloaded. The Ball canning company publishes a "Blue Book" for canning which is a reliable guide with many recipes and is usually available where canning supplies are sold. There are also many recipes and guides at your local library. To make canning safe, be sure to update the safety information using current guidelines. Varieties of produce change which may affect the acid level of your produce. Current guidelines will help you decide the best method of canning.

Section IV
Eat Well

Chapter 32: Enjoy!

For centuries, food has been recognized for its sensory qualities. Nature has teased us with the sight and smells of food to entice our eating and therefore, proliferation of foods through pleasure. Food is used to heal, nourish, seduce and celebrate, assuring that pleasure and company keeps our food system and us alive.

Our strongest memories are associated with the taste and smell of food, often shared with people we love or as gestures of how much we love ourselves. Learning a family recipe, growing your family's heirloom seeds, developing food rituals such as holiday baking and birthday celebrations, and showing gratitude for the daily meal, are ways we demonstrate our relationship with food. Food rituals, large and small, keep our heritage alive for generations.

Growing up, my siblings and I would stay overnight at our great-aunt's house, a tradition that I continued throughout college and into adulthood with my children. My Aunt Cel had a rhythm about life and meals, which included a properly set table, a whistling teakettle and a prayer before and after the meal. One of my earliest memories as a child at her house is learning to wait for the little bubbles on top of pancakes to pop before flipping, or walking to the shoreline for the afternoon with lunch packed in the Radio Flyer wagon. Visiting as a college student, I woke to her humming and the teakettle singing. Food memories help define our families and our cultures.

Food is one of the social building blocks in our community. Families come from rich heritages which saved seeds, utilized plants for nourishment and healing, and practiced food preservation and thriftiness. In our area, Polish immigrants used their knowledge of mushrooms to forage in the local areas; yet as foraging has diminished, this skill may be fast disappearing. Food festivals keep local food culture alive while making lasting memories for the whole community.

Simple Steps to Celebrate Food

🍎 Have elders talk about the food they enjoyed when growing up.

🍎 Learn about the people that settled in your community and the new food they brought with them.

🍎 Think about your food rituals or family celebrations and who influenced these.

🍎 Have everyone talk about their favorite foods during each season and make a plan to visit a farmers' market or grocery store to find these throughout the year.

🍎 Teach a younger family member to cook a favorite meal.

🍎 Go to the farmers' market with a picnic basket and plan a place to eat afterwards.

🍎 Participate in local food festivals in your area and learn the local food heritage.

🍎 Pay attention to presentation: Use color, order and ritual to make meals more inviting.

Chapter 33: Cooking Tips

Cooking is much easier with local ingredients. How can I be so sure of this when we are told that meal preparation is long and difficult? The truth is that starting with quality ingredients makes every dish taste great. Chefs know this and strive to present the food at its best rather than mask the natural taste of food. Only poor quality food needs to be smothered with sauces, seasonings, ketchup or breading. Good cooking is simple, quick and easy. Learning to cook not only saves money but gives you more flexibility for ingredients.

Planning a meal. Start with basic items already in your pantry and add fresh ingredients to make meals easy and inexpensive. Visit your garden, farmers' market or produce section of the grocery store to find fresh, local food. For instance, any pasta or rice dish is perked up with a fresh vegetable. A simple dessert of yogurt with fresh blackberries or blueberries becomes a treat.

Variety will naturally occur with local, seasonal foods. The first vegetables to appear are the quick growing, cool tolerant greens, small bulbs, and tubers such as radish, turnips and potatoes. Use these raw or cooked, as side dishes or salads, or combined in the main entrée. Different harvest times provide different flavors over the year, so think about flavor and texture variation when you use local produce.

Meals are satisfying to the palate if they appeal to the senses. My mother often says, "You eat with your eyes first." Plates with too much or too little color are off-putting. Just the right combination of color adds interest and appeal. Vegetable and fruits stay vibrant in a raw salad, gently steamed or quickly stir-fried.

Compliment flavors and experiment with spices and herbs – having a small pot of herbs handy encourages this. The flavor in vegetables can be accentuated or muted when raw versus cooked; don't be afraid to experiment with these flavors.

Vary the textures within a meal. You can add crisp and crunch with a raw dish such as crudités (raw vegetables and dipping sauce), salads or fermented foods. Creaminess can come from sauces, cheese or beans. Leaves of vegetables add a different texture compared to the stems.

"Mise en place." A French term for thinking, planning and organizing a meal is "mise en place" or "everything in its place". Develop quick methods for preparing meals and enjoyable ways to cook with family and friends as you ready everything in your kitchen before you start the actual cooking. Read the recipe thoroughly, checking for ingredients or substitutes and visualizing the preparation. Reading the recipe will help you plan for the actual cooking time.

Divide the work in a recipe over time so that when you come home from work, some of the preparation is finished. Beans and grains can be prepared a few days ahead of the meal – double the recipe and then freeze a portion for another day. Prepare grains for one meal and then use them also as part of a salad or stir-fry later in the week.

When you are ready to cook, first take out all your ingredients and equipment. Next, complete all the preparation steps including washing, peeling and cutting vegetables. When a friend was teaching me new Indian dishes, we spent the first ten minutes cutting all the vegetables and putting them in different plates or bowls. This preparation made the cooking very fast and efficient. As she stir-fried, she quickly reached for the next ingredient, recognizing minced foods will cook very quickly while larger cuts take longer, so she could easily control the cooking process. You can change the flavor of a dish by changing the cut of the vegetable. A smaller cut will increase the surface area of the vegetable so it will cook quickly and absorb more flavors. Different cuts also add visual interest to a dish.

In our house, we follow a basic meal pattern. The base of our meal is a grain with vegetables. The grain may be pasta, rice or bulgur. We enjoy onions and garlic and typically start with a sauté of these; add the vegetables that are ripe; drop in flavorings such as spices, herbs or a cube of frozen pesto; add nuts, seeds or cooked beans, and serve over the grain. We accompany this with a raw dish, bread and an occasional slice of cheese. The different vegetables with combinations of spices and herbs add enough variety that this basic plan is never repetitive and takes only 20-30 minutes.

Simple cooking techniques. Quality ingredients need only simple cooking techniques. A little water in a pan will quickly steam vegetables; add a bit of oil and you can pan-fry or turn up the heat to stir-fry. Roasting may take an hour but if your mise en place is very simple, just add a variety of vegetables, and meat if you choose, and bake. Crock pots have simplified cooking and makes opening the door after work a treat as the smells have filled your kitchen.

Presentation. Preparation is not complete until you present the meal. Celebrating a meal is a daily occurrence; even the simplest meal is special when you present the food attractively. Clearing the table; setting the place with plates, glasses and silverware; and serving your meal in bowls rather than pots, are signals that a meal is worthwhile and eating is nourishing.

Community. Make cooking a social event. Sunday afternoon cooking with friends provides an easy workload, enjoyable conversations, and meals for the next week. Sharing family recipes provides more variety.

Chapter 34: Slow Food

There is a growing movement around the world to celebrate the many aspects of food and farming, and protect our heritage for future generations. The Slow Food movement is an effort to keep food traditions alive, protect local ecosystems and pass knowledge to the next generation. The movement began as a reaction to a McDonald's opening near the Piazza di Spagna in Rome in 1986. Carlo Petrini organized a demonstration which included flaunting penne pasta in protest of the fast food. In order to promote corporate homogenization and industrialized foods, fast food franchising was pushing unique, locally-owned restaurants out of business. Today, Slow Food is an international organization with small groups called "conviviums" located around the world. The U.S. has more than 200 local chapters, with one or more in each state. Above all, Slow Food celebrates food as the center of culture and community with an emphasis on pleasurable eating.

Slow Food has become a symbol of food culture. The conviviums are centered on food celebrations that are specific to a community, help preserve a healthy environment, and support an equitable food system. Local food production techniques such as regional cheese making, vegetable pickling, and wild rice harvesting and processing, are preserved through teaching and eating. The movement  supports cultural food celebrations; encourages finding your neighbors who have knowledge of unique foods that grow in gardens, farms or wild areas, and emphasizes the unique rather than the common. In this way, groups hope to preserve food heritage around the world and support biodiversity of species. Food conversations are encouraged with classes, dinners, events and speakers. Communities begin to recognize the wealth of food connections and people who have unique food knowledge. The end result is a lively group of people who encourage local farmers, sustainable food production, family food education, and a healthy environment.

Like many Europeans and middle-aged Americans, I grew up with an inflexible dinner time. All the children knew that we were to be home for dinner when Dad would get home from work – the only ex-  ception was school sports or drama. This regular dinner hour established a routine in our family with lively conversation (sometimes too lively for Mom and Dad), table etiquette, a relaxed atmosphere to eat nourishing food, and daily chores of setting a table and cleaning up. While this may sound familiar to sitcom viewers of 1950s programs, this was a welcomed break to see my family before rushing off for homework or friends. It was a dependable routine for a group of busy people who often prefer individual lives rather than family identity while growing up. This predated the Slow Food movement but my parents' efforts to teach us about family through our dinner time would nicely fit. For my own children, we adapted the family dinner time to suit our lifestyles, eating later in the evening, while enjoying the same rhythm of mealtimes.

In contrast to the message in modern times of cooking as onerous, meals as interruptions or wayside experiences and food as forgettable, the Slow Food movement encourages each person to decide the value of food and recognize the pleasures of eating with other people. The shared experience of eating encourages a slower pace, makes the meal a welcomed break in our day, and fosters connections between people. Food as pleasurable fosters a creative and curious view of food, creating food memories and knowledge.

Special mention should be made about the Slow Food Foundation for Biodiversity. This organization recognizes groups of producers who have a product at risk of extinction. These producers may use a traditional process or agricultural method at risk of disappearing or produce a local plant or breed that may become extinct or lost to corporate patent laws. For instance, the United States had 15,000 distinct apple varieties in the past century, apples that varied in texture, color, size, aroma and taste. These apples were available locally and served many purposes with families familiar with grafting, pruning, processing and eating a wide variety of apples. This has dwindled to the eleven varieties that contribute 90% of our apple production and consumption today.

Slow Food USA has recognized this disappearance with a campaign to teach apple production and support the resurgence of American apple varieties that are still available. This work is being done by growers and consumers across our country, not researchers and scientists, since this work is part of backyard trees and farms. Apples and other food varieties and breeds are slowly being identified; producers are encouraged to keep heritage stock productive, and consumers are asked to support these efforts. You may ask your local farmer about special breeds or varieties since she can give you specific information about the food characteristics and tips for preparation or storage. It is exciting for children to try different types of foods and many favorites are discovered.

Simple Steps to Enjoy Slow Food

🍅 Celebrate eating together.

🍅 Enjoy the food you find in your own community; be willing to try new foods.

🍅 Ask an elderly person about the food ways of their life including food they had eaten, food preparation and food celebrations. You can often find a food heritage within your own family by showing interest in these stories.

🍅 Find a Slow Food conviviums close to you by searching the website, www.slowfoodusa.org.

🍅 Discover native plants and breeds in your area by speaking with growers at farmers' markets or employees at seed stores.

🍅 Eat foods from heirloom plants and breeds to maintain biodiversity in our food system.

🍅 Check www.localharvest.org to find those foods at risk of extinction that are grown near you

Chapter 35: Organic Food

Organic food is increasingly available in grocery stores, farmers' markets and farms. In the last two decades, organic agriculture acreage has doubled and organic food sales have more than quintupled. While organics grow in popularity, there is also confusion about organic versus local foods, often mistakenly used interchangeably. Perhaps contributing to this confusion is the thirty-year growth of organic agriculture as a local movement in various states before becoming a national food option.

Is organic new? Organic food production is not a new phenomena but a resurgence of past farming methods with new understandings of resources such as soil ecosystems. Before the creation of synthetic chemicals, most food production was organic which depended on biological or physical methods such as compost, manure and hand weeding to support healthy plant growth. The developments in plant breeding, tractor production, inexpensive oil, synthetic fertilizer and pesticides expanded the ability of farmers to cultivate larger fields efficiently and affordably. This also led to the industrialization of farming. We entered the age of technology and chemicals in farming with the philosophy of bigger farms and fewer farmers.

The synthetic chemicals, fertilizers and pesticides used today were created from World War II technologies; for instance, many of the pesticides evolved from the nerve gas and fertilizer from ammonium nitrate used in munitions. There were short-term benefits of using these chemicals with increased production and a uniform product. We could not only feed ourselves but also export food around the world.

Not everyone, however, accepted these new production methods. In 1942, Jerome Rodale began printing the "Organic Farming and Gardening" magazine that is still in print today. A small group of people promoted organic farming methods while most of society welcomed the new chemicals until 1962, when biologist Rachel Carson published *Silent Spring*, which exposed the negative effects of DDT, leading to its ban and prompting questions about the effect of chemicals on the environment. The 1970s began a period of expanding organic farming which continues today.

What makes organic different than conventional? Originally, organic food production was seen as part of a larger sustainable food movement that includes not only organic agriculture but supports economic development and social benefits. According to the Organic Trade Association, "organic food production is based on a system of farming that maintains and replenishes soil fertility without the use of toxic and persistent pesticides and fertilizers. Organic foods are minimally processed without artificial ingredients, preservatives, or irradiation to maintain the integrity of the food."

What is certified organic? "Certified Organic" means the item is grown according to strict uniform standards approved by the National Organics Standards Board and verified by independent state or private organizations. (Search the www.usda.gov website for organics). Organics are grown around the world, so organic food in the grocery store may or may not be locally grown. It is important to note that certification limits the definition of organic to agricultural production and does not address economic or social equity.

Will it cost more? Organic foods prices compared to conventional food prices vary by the type of food, the market where you purchase organic food and whether you buy whole or processed. The more processed the food, including organic food with organic ingredients, the higher the cost you pay for marketing, processing and packaging. Organic food may also have a higher price with the increased labor that farmers use instead of chemicals to control weeds and pests. Additionally, organic agriculture requires extensive record-keeping with every input recorded and yearly inspections. Farmers are charged a fee for certification.

Are there health benefits of eating organic? The major benefit of organic production lies in reduced pesticide exposure, especially in children. Decreased pesticides also keep our water and soil safe for generations. While we have just started to study the nutritional benefits of organic food, early studies either show some nutritional advantage in a few nutrients or no differences.

"Dirty Dozen"

Each year the Environmental Working Group (www.foodnews.org) determines the foods with the highest and lowest in pesticide residue.

1. Apples
2. Celery
3. Strawberries
4. Peaches
5. Spinach
6. Nectarines - imported
7. Grapes - imported
8. Sweet bell peppers
9. Potatoes
10. Blueberries - domestic
11. Lettuce
12. Kale / collard greens

Chapter 36:
Sustainable Food

There is a change in the wind and if you are reading this book, you are one of the many people who suspect that the current methods of growing, processing and distributing our food are not sustainable. We cannot have a small handful of large companies dictate our food supply. We cannot depend on distant places of the world to grow our food, sacrificing their land and water so we can eat out-of-season strawberries, peas or broccoli. We cannot see rural communities wither because new farmers cannot afford farmland and older farmers cannot retire without losing their investment. Nor can we continue to have families, especially our children, have diets that depend on cheap food that is unhealthy. A sustainable food system provides for the needs of the current population without jeopardizing the needs of future generations.

Building community. Sustainable food production considers humans as a vital resource, supporting fair and safe working conditions for farmers, farm workers and food processors. It also supports the rural culture so that farmers can live in places that support food production while keeping rural culture intact. Healthy rural communities include an agricultural economy that can support local grocery stores, hardware stores, schools, churches and other services. Human resources also include a fair wage for both producing and processing affordable food.

Simple Steps to Build Community

- Celebrate and support local food culture.

- Find and talk to local farmers: Recognize their knowledge and skills and learn where your food comes from.

- Support fair prices for food and fair wages for farmers and farm workers.

- Build local markets for local food to strengthen the local economy and keep rural communities vibrant.

Reinvest in farming. We are facing a dilemma of farming within the United States as the average age of the farmers has continued to climb, now at 57.1 years and less than 0.05% of our population is farmers (www.numberof.net/number-of-farmers-in-us). U.S. agriculture production is dominated by large farms, i.e., farms with gross sales of $250,000 or more. These farms contribute 80% of the value of production although smaller farms own 63% of the farmland. This concentration of market dominance by larger farms prevents midsized farms from increasing their market share.

Large production also leads to the increased dependence on large machinery and monocropping, i.e., planting one continuous crop on many acres. These practices lead to decreased soil health and increased crop diseases. For many reasons, supporting a market with more farmers and diversified farms supports local communities, a safer food supply and a healthier ecosystem.

Simple Steps to Reinvest in Farming

- Support grocery stores and farmer's markets that buy from regional farmers.

- Localize the food in your schools, hospitals and other institutions – encourage a "buy local" food clause in food contracts.

- Retain the zoning of agricultural land rather than land development and lobby for a tax base favorable for agricultural development.

- Keep public land available for farmers' markets, school gardens and community gardens so everyone in your community knows about agriculture.

- Increase your purchases of local food and encourage local food in community celebrations, family events and social gatherings.

- Call on your national political representatives to end farm subsidies.

Use resources responsibly. Recent historians have suggested that past cultures have disappeared because of damage to their natural resources. Three resources are vital for successful agriculture and are currently disappearing in our country at alarming levels: soil, water and seeds.

We need to pay closer attention to soil health as we have been losing topsoil each year, compromising our future food supply. According to the U.S. Department of Agriculture, keeping soil healthy as a living organism requires simple steps: don't disturb the soil; keep soil covered; provide diversity; keep living roots in the soil; and don't compact the soil.

Monitoring water quality and quantity is essential for our survival. It is critical to decrease chemicals that contribute to pollution and affect communities who live downstream. Increased attention to water leads to increased monitoring of use, improved irrigation techniques and better soil management. We must also hold the food system accountable for maintaining quality water within local aquifers.

Current trends threaten our ability to have a diverse seed stock. The increased dependence on hybrid seeds results in a decline of traditional seeds that provide the genetic diversity needed to develop resistant strains. The ability of companies to own patent rights to seeds means taking seeds, freely traded around the world, into corporate control. Finally, there is increased planting of genetically modified organisms (GMO) without understanding the consequences to the natural world. Cross-contamination and disease resistance has been found with some GMO crops, which threatens farmers' livelihoods and natural biodiversity.

Simple Steps to Use Resources Responsibly

- Farmers will plant diverse crops if purchased. Buy a variety of foods and support local food in your stores and farmers' markets.

- Support low carbon agriculture that follows nature's principles such as no-till, biodynamic and organic agriculture practices.

- Reduce your consumption of foods from animals and support animal welfare standards.

- Use all the food you buy; compost plant scraps, and reuse bags – these steps reduce water and energy usage through decreased packaging and processing.

- Know where your water comes from, where it goes and how to keep water healthy and local.

- Learn how to maintain healthy soil in your yard, gardens and surrounding landscape.

- Save seeds, trade seeds and attract insect pollinators to your garden. Go to www.seedsavers.com to learn more.

- Ask for stricter regulations of GMO crops and resist the release of GMO seeds without further studies.

Chapter 37: Animal Options

Animal production is often idyllically portrayed in marketing as cows or chickens freely roaming the fields, foraging for food. Consumers would be surprised to find that they may regularly pass farms with large numbers livestock hidden from view. My commute to work takes me past a number of buildings holding hundreds of pigs who are never outside; the only indication is the smell when the wind blows in my direction.

The vast majority of meat production is an example of maximizing industrial efficiency beyond reason with unsafe consequences. Current meat production practices raise animal to market with the least amount of inputs, in the fastest time, with maximum profits. This has led to a dominance of concentrated animal feedlot operations (CAFO) – small, restricted areas where grass or other plants are unavailable. That is, animals are unable to graze and are on bedding or manure. All feed is brought to the animals and excrement is removed.

A large animal operation is typically more than 1,000 cattle, 2,500 swine or 125,000 chickens. Historically, there is a limit to the number of animals on land because of the balance between the fields of grass for grazing or growing feed grain. These same fields would then be spread

with manure that replaces the lost nitrogen. But in animal feeding operations, this carrying capacity of the land is exceeded. The small space does not have adequate grazing land and the amount of manure generated is toxic to the land. Squeezing so many animals into small areas also has a number of other problems.

Concern about the quality of meat from large production and processing facilities, the control of the meat industry by a handful of companies and the ethical and humanitarian issues of animals raised in small spaces without access to the outdoors and workers in extremely dangerous meat-packing facilities have led some consumers to seek meat or eggs from small-scale, local farmers who use alternative production methods.

Farmers who pasture small herds of animals cite the relative environmental and nutrient benefits of raising grass-fed animals compared to large-scale animal production methods. Consumers who support these local farmers are willing to pay the higher cost of pastured meat or local eggs. Especially since the recent egg-salmonella outbreak and increasing egg prices, many communities, too, are revisiting city laws to allow egg and small animal production.

Pastured animals and birds. Allowing animals and birds to be outdoors recognizes their natural behaviors necessary for health such as pecking, scratching, rooting, wallowing, socializing, or nesting. They are natural foragers and need diversity in their diet, including various grasses, insects or weeds. Pasturing has agricultural and environmental benefits for maintaining plant diversity and soil health. Cattle and sheep are ruminants with stomachs designed to ferment grass for nutrients. Eating grass rather than grain maintains their natural, healthy bacteria and prevents the growth of harmful bacteria. Animals also need exposure to sunlight for vitamin D production, just like humans.

Biodiversity. Animal breeds are adapted to different pasture conditions and local environments. Like plants, consolidation has led to an alarming decline in breeds with risks of becoming extinct; we have already lost 190 breeds of farm animals within the past 15 years. Currently the majority of livestock production involves three to five main breeds. Animals and plants interact to maintain a biodiverse ecosystem; we are destroying breeds before understanding this relationship. Your local farmer may keep heritage breeds and biodiversity alive, ensuring that valuable genetic traits are preserved, which may be essential as environmental conditions change.

Antibiotics and Hormones. Confining animals in close quarters is a disease risk, as any outbreak would spread quickly and kill many other animals. Therefore, antibiotics are routinely added to the feed. This routine antibiotic use has led to antibiotic resistant strains now threatening the human population. The medical community recommends giving antibiotics only if the animals are sick. If farmers are contracted by companies, then the feed is predetermined and may include these chemicals. Independent farmers with small herds or pastured animals can often avoid using antibiotics unless the animal is ill.

Artificial growth hormones are given to livestock and dairy cows. Two genetically engineered hormones, recombinant bovine growth hormone (rBGH) and recombinant bovine somatotropin (rBST) are most prominent in the U.S. dairy industry but not allowed in the European Union or Canada and other countries. Labeling laws vary from state to state regarding the ability to label milk as rBST- or rBGH-free.

Organic. There are specific rules that govern animal production by the Department of Agriculture. These rules include access to the outside, provision of organic feed, and processing restrictions. Animals may not be given antibiotics, growth hormones, steroids or genetically modified feed.

Cost. The cost of animal products does not reflect the true cost of production: consumers pay for subsidizing grain, decreased property values near confined animal operations, human health  costs, and pollution abatement. Communities can hold the meat industry and legislatures accountable for this and support alternatives. Animals without grain, by-products or drugs grow slower. This, combined with smaller herds, impacts the price of the meat. Fewer animals are healthier animals and reduce the impact on the environment. This higher cost of production reflects the true cost of food production.

Transition to local & hormone free. Because of the higher cost of meat from grass-fed animals, most consumers of locally-purchased meat use smaller portions in their cooking. They often state that the taste of organic, grass-fed meat may satisfy their taste in smaller portions. Other consumers choose to reduce meat for additional reasons – see next chapter.

Because of the concentration of the meat industry, these farmers are under pressure to raise animals and birds quickly and cheaply, causing risk to both animals and humans. Breeds that favor local conditions, consideration of the limits of land capacity, and inno-  vative production techniques have resulted from farmers desiring a more equitable system and consumers paying attention to their food. The food system changes when the farmer and customer can directly support each other. Know your farmer and ask questions. If you have doubts, ask to visit the farm.

Animal Options:
Questions to ask farmers

- Are your animals or chickens raised on pasture? If so, how long?

- What are your animals or chickens fed?

- Are your animals or chickens ever given nontherapeutic antibiotics?

- Are hormones, steroids, or other growth promoters fed to your animals or birds (includes any premixed in commercial feed)?

- How much time do your animals or chickens spend outdoors each day?

- Where were your animals or chickens born?

- Do you raise heritage breeds?

Chapter 38: The Plant-Based Diet

The majority of the world consumes a plant-based diet stemming from the intensive resources, including land and water, needed to raise animals (whether feedlot- or grass-fed), and the resulting higher price. Since animal products are more expensive, many cuisines throughout the world focus on plant-based foods, and even in cuisines that include meat, plant-based diets are the mainstay of the meal.

In the U.S., too, people are reducing their meat consumption out of choice or necessity. Many local food advocates, trying to find other options besides the factory-farm meat products are generally looking at two directions: Eating less meat and purchasing local, hormone-free (previous chapter), or reducing or eliminating meat consumption through a plant-based diet.

Expense. The recent economic slump has made many home cooks look for ways to stretch their food dollars, including buying less meat. Reducing expensive meat consumption is one of the quickest ways to reduce your food costs. Beans are versatile and inexpensive, with local varieties available. Gradually increase bean consumption so your gut adjusts and flatulence is avoided.

Health. While meat is nutrient rich, it is also calorie dense and excessive amounts lead to weight gain and disease risk. Given the recent fast food menus with ever increasing amounts of meat, it is small wonder obesity has become a national epidemic. When

large burgers were introduced, the quarter pounder seemed excessive and is now dwarfed by the one-third, and incredibly, two-thirds pound of meat in a fast food sandwich.

Recent official U.S. government dietary recommendations advocate a predominantly plant-based diet for health reasons. Plant-based diets are typically low in fat and high in fiber with varied vegetables and fruits. Vegetarians have lower risks of heart disease and some cancers.

As a dietitian, many people ask me about the adequacy of vegetarian diets with specific concerns. If you are consuming enough calories, eat a varied diet with whole grains, beans, nuts or seeds, your protein intake will be adequate. Two nutrients deserve attention, vitamin B-12 and iron. Vitamin B-12 is only found in animal products (including dairy) so if your diet excludes these, include foods fortified with this vitamin or take a supplement. The form of iron in meat is readily absorbed by the body, while plant forms of iron have lower absorption rates. Pair vitamin C-rich foods with iron-rich foods to help absorption such as oranges with spinach or tomatoes and lentils.

Environmental. A large portion of our resources is used for feeding livestock. A pound of beef requires 1860 gallons of water and three-quarters of a gallon of oil. Livestock also contributes more to global warming and greenhouse-gas emissions than transportation. The same resources could instead be used to grow cheaper, less resource-intensive grains and other foods with fewer environmental impacts. To benefit from switching to a plant based diet, consider organic produce which decreases our carbon footprint and saves water. Find farmers that practice sustainable agriculture, such as permaculture.

Compassion. Those who advocate less or no meat generally point out that the rise in meat consumption in recent decades in affluent countries has come hand in hand with the distance modern  consumers are from their food supply. It is easy to forget, or not consider, that the meat that comes wrapped from the grocery store also comes from living animals. Compassionate actions may include reducing meat in your diet. Each time you eat, you are supporting a specific food system. Knowing all aspects of where your food comes from supports your ability to make ethical decisions.

Transition. Changing from a meat centered American diet to one with less meat can be a challenge given the sparse use of herbs and spices in our typical cuisine. These condiments, like meat, trigger our fifth taste, umami, and without them, this savory taste can be left unsatisfied. Adding foods that trigger umami, such as ripe tomatoes, aged cheeses, soy sauce and  mushrooms, satisfies this taste. When I transitioned into eating less meat, I adopted my "Wisconsin vegetarian diet", substituting cheese and milk for any meat that I had been eating. While it was tasty, it was not satisfying and I tired of the meals. Fortunately, the global village has developed cuisines that are abundant in plant-based cooking. My friends Rekha and Fizza, introduced me to Indian cooking, with the art of spicing and the ability to use beans in a wide variety of ways – this opened my eyes to more satisfying vegetarian cooking.

I was fortunate to stay with a family who were vegetarian for generations. I was amazed at the variety of dishes, the combination of flavors and the complete satisfaction of the meal. The local library has well-developed cooking sections from around the world. Many communities offer cooking classes in various world cuisines introducing the basics of their cooking.

Simple Steps
to a Plant-Based Diet

Reduce meat portions in meal planning.

Choose whole grains rather than refined to boost flavor and health.

Eat an abundance of beans, nuts and seeds.

Eat a variety of foods every day. Shopping at the farmers' market and eating seasonally makes this easy.

Enjoy the many cuisines around the world that feature vegetarian cooking.

Learn to cook with herbs and spices to satisfy the savory taste.

Add mushrooms and other foods that trigger umami, the fifth taste, to dishes such as soups and casseroles to satisfy this savory taste.

If you avoid meat products entirely, eat foods fortified with vitamin B-12 or take a supplement.

Section V
Join the Local Food Movement

Chapter 39: Investing in Our Children

Investing in the children of our nation is a priority and a responsibility. The good news about local food is that children are excited to be involved with their food. A recent Berkeley California school initiative involved fourth and fifth graders in a school garden, cooking classes and an integration of food into the curriculum. Children exposed to this innovative program had better knowledge of healthy choices and food attitudes along with higher consumption of fruits and vegetables. The bottom line is that when adults involve children in knowing about their food and celebrating this food, they are healthier and smarter about food.

Children reach their capacity of growth and learning when they have good food. The recent changes, largely unplanned, away from real wholesome food into a highly processed food system abundant in sugar and fat, has resulted not only in overweight and obese children but serious health consequences for their future.

Families and communities decide what type of food our children see and eat every day. If we surround our children with only food in the grocery store or only processed food, then they will not connect the food they eat with nature or the farmers. Where will children learn about food? Who will teach them? How will extended families and communities support food education for our children? Anyone taking a short trip down the supermarket aisle to see how food is marketed, realizes that our runaway food system does not have our children's well-being in mind. Collectively, we can reinforce positive food values for children by providing wholesome food in our homes, neighborhoods and communities. If we do a better job producing food with that does not damage our soils, pollute our water or strip away natural nutrition, then better eating will result. With simple steps, we can provide a healthy, joyful food environment for all children.

Support garden spaces. Whether in personal or public spaces, gardens can surround children and demonstrate simple ways to grow food. Start a window garden with your children: Your front or back yard, rooftop or porch and windowsills are all personal spaces for container or ground gardens. Community gardens and school gardens are increasing and these spaces must be supported by everyone with public zoning, supportive tax structures, or community maintenance. The more we surround children with gardens, the more we reinforce the joy of growing our own food.

Meet the farmer. With less than one percent of Americans claiming farming as an occupation, farmers are disappearing from our communities, making farmers' markets the perfect place to meet the people producing our food. Enable your children to experience farm life by picking your own food at U-pick farms, or by visiting a local organic farm. Children not only are able to taste fruits or vegetables right from their plants but also see the farm. Studies show that children are more likely to eat food if they are somehow involved in its process, so harvesting creates strong memories of sight, smell and taste.

Lobby for good food. Whether it is your child's daycare, public and private schools, or community festivals, we can reinforce good food through regulations, policies and public support. Help to educate people on food safe practices that also encourage wholesome, local food so children will experience fresh, nutritious food everywhere. Keep abreast of legal and cultural changes that affect our local food.

Three national bills – Food, Conservation, and Energy Act of 2008 (aka "the farm bill"); the Child Nutrition Reauthorization bill – which account for much of the funding for our current food system; and the recently passed the FDA Food Safety Modernization Act – determine our ability to provide equitable food choices and food production. We need to hold legislatures responsible for supporting a food system that protects the safety of our children and the environment. Education curriculum and school meals can reinforce food knowledge for all children. Vote for local zoning ordinances and tax structures that support local agriculture land and farmer's markets. Our actions to support local food will ensure that it will be here for many generations of children.

Chapter 40: Join a Local Food Group

In 2005, a group of San Francisco women named themselves locavores and challenged residents to eat locally for one month. Enthusiasts joined in and the campaign spread nationwide. Now an accepted word, "locavore" is a person who prefers to eat locally grown food within 100 miles of their home.

Identifying local food producers, finding new cooking strategies, and encouraging more local food in your community may often be challenging or frustrating. Finding a group can change eating local into a celebration. Local foodies swap food tips and connect within communities or online. There are many benefits to knowing others involved in local food, sharing knowledge and supporting change.

A surprising number of people are already involved in the local food movement. A few years ago in our area, a small group held a state local food summit, inviting supporters they knew. The summit grew to a few hundred people and is now an annual event in Wisconsin. We spend two days listening to speakers, sharing novel strategies and eating delicious local food. Farmers feel supported by this energetic group and we all feel that change is possible.

To find those in your area, look for events that involve local food. Watch the local paper for events about local food processing or events such as food preservation workshops, local food fairs, film showings or garden tours. Ask the local extension agent or food co-op about local groups or search the internet for "local food challenge" with the name of your community or state.

Many blogs and websites discuss local food issues. Check out the Resources page at this book's web site, www.eatlocalsimplesteps.com. Also look at Sustainable Table (www.sustainabletable.org), which has information about sustainable food choices that include local eating strategies. Farm Aid (www.farmaid.org) also has valuable local food movement resources, and their Farmer Resource Network helps connect farmers to organizations and websites involved with many aspects of growing, processing and marketing local food.

Slow Food, an international organization that celebrates local food, has local chapters that celebrate the heritage foods, sustainable farmers and cooking skills in your area. Check out their website, www.slowfoodusa.org, for the closest chapter.

Simple Steps to Join a Local Food Group

MEMO: Meeting Today

- Check your local newspaper or weekly for local food events; notice who is sponsoring the event and try to attend.

- Ask your local extension agent about local food groups in your area.

- Your community regional food guide, which lists farmers, farmers' markets and businesses, alerts you to others interested in local food. See who is producing the guide and volunteer your efforts.

- Join other food- or homesteading-related, online social networking groups to share stories and tips, such as Homegrown.org and kitchengardeners.org

Chapter 41: School Gardens

School gardens provide a living classroom where students gain valuable skills about working together in a natural setting to produce valuable and essential food. What better place to learn about food than in the schools, where children spend the majority of their youth? The intellectual, physical and sensory stimulation found in the garden engenders lifelong skills and disciplines, including math, science, ecology, English, nutrition and geography. There are a number of innovative programs already available for schools and many reliable resources to get any school started and progressing in local food education.

Research has shown that when children grow their food and then taste it, their food habits change. These children develop a favorable attitude toward fruit and vegetable consumption at both school and home. They also consume more fruits and vegetables compared to children who do not garden and prepare garden food.

A garden requires a dedicated group both within and beyond the school to ensure success. Preparing, planting and maintaining a garden may require attention year-round, even when school is not in session. In some growing zones, a productive time of the garden may be during the summer break when only a handful of students or teachers are active in the school.

There are spark plugs for every change. Parents, teachers, administrators are often these energetic visionaries. Your involvement and support is important for providing a gardening opportunity in your neighborhood school. You can speak with the school administrator or a teacher about establishing a school garden. If a garden exists at your neighborhood school, inquire about volunteer activities.

Successful gardens have a sustainable stream of resources including seeds, tools, compost, fencing, etc. If a school is willing to dedicate land to a garden project, administrators want assurance that a core group of volunteers will design, build and maintain the garden throughout the  years. Ask local gardening centers and hardware stores to be partners in the project. Community gardening groups such as Master Gardeners or your county extension office can provide expertise.

Simple Steps: School Gardens

Identify a suitable space. This implies adequate sunlight, lack of debris, and adequate water.

Seek approval of administration. This is necessary to help rally the community and the rest of the school.

Find an enthusiastic teacher. This is the most important factor since an eager teacher will work with the children successfully while inspiring other teachers.

Gather resources for supplies. This may be donations, sponsors or a designated budget. You need a reliable source of income or supplies for the garden to be sustainable.

Organize a small, dedicated core of volunteers. There will be many tasks, including designing the garden, preparing the space, collecting supplies and maintaining the garden.

Chapter 42: Farm to School Programs

Strengthening the knowledge and connection between agriculture and schools builds a strong base for children to learn about healthy food. For the past decade, many schools have started innovative programs that bring farmers, school personnel and students together. Teachers and school food service directors report the excitement that children have in discovering their food. One director recently told me that the children had grown used to the local apple varieties served during lunch and were disappointed when they had to eat apples ordered from across the nation. As education about food and food production has declined within the home, schools have become important institutions to fill this gap.

The Farm to School program began in 1996 and grew to a national movement. The programs vary from school to school, often collaborating with local farmers, increasing local farm food in the school meal programs, establishing school gardens, introducing cooking classes that incorporate local food and teaching healthy eating habits with whole foods. You can find information about the USDA supported programs and available grants at www.fns.usda.gov/cnd/f2s/default.htm.

Your school may have teams focused on improving the food choices within the school environment. Team Nutrition and the wellness team assess and plan changes to improve the food environment throughout classrooms, lunchroom and school events. Both teams can support the Farm to School program's efforts to incorporate healthy food and food education.

Simple Steps to Support Farm to School Programs

- *Find out more.* Ask about school programs that support healthy food such as school wellness policies, farm to school programs, or Team Nutrition.

- *Buy local.* Encourage local food in many venues at school. Bringing local fruits into a snack program or vending machines, local vegetables during school lunch or local food fundraisers are all projects that have been done successfully in schools.

- *Vote yes!* Support partnerships between local farmers and local school.

- *Meet the school food service director.* The director is responsible for the menu and purchasing in school meal programs. She can explain the current regulations and fiscal constraints in your school and provide suggestions for supporting improved food and nutrition.

- *Encourage teachers and administrators.* Teachers integrate local food into their curriculum successfully when supported by the community, especially the parents. Curriculums are available to meet standards for education so teachers do not have to create their own.

- *Get involved.* Volunteer to promote local food activities. Community assistance in taste testing, school gardens, fund-raisers and farmer communication will support change in your schools.

- *Learn more.* You can support the work done at the schools by supporting local food at home and in your community. Strong local food networks strengthen each other.

- *Celebrate successes.* Announce each small step that you make toward healthier eating with news stories, pictures and notes to administrators and community members.

- *See www.farmtoschool.org* for more information and resources.

Chapter 43: Helping the Hungry

Eating whole foods fresh from the farmers is nourishing for everyone. There are a number of ways local food is able to reach people with highest risk. More than 40 percent of food produced in the United States is wasted. Each year, more than 130 pounds of food per person ends up in landfills. We can recover food from the field, from wholesale or retail outlets, after processing in either perishable or nonperishable forms. All along the food chain, food is wasted; yet programs exist to collect and incorporate this food into programs for the hungry.

Gleaning allows people to go into fields after the mechanical harvesting to pick the produce missed by the machine. The farmer donates the produce and hungry people can eat food picked within 48 hours of harvest. The Society of St. Andrew, with gleaning programs in more than 30 states, is a very successful example, harvesting more than 15 million pounds of produce.

Our local nonprofit community group circles the farmers' market near the end of the day, collecting produce donated by farmers. This quick food recovery requires only two people, a wagon and car for transportation. The hungry are able to eat fresh produce and a healthy seasonal diet.

The Bill Emerson Good Samaritan Food Donation Act limits the liability of donors and allays the concerns of those involved in recovering food. State Good Samaritan laws may further protect gleaners and donors from liability.

Food recovery saves the community in several ways; local food is utilized rather than plowed under, maximizing the resources used in food production. Food recovered reduces food in the garbage and landfills. Most importantly, recovering local food helps a community feed its people.

Simple Steps for Food Recovery

- Locate the food. Small and large operations may have food to donate. Think about each stop along the food chain and identify recovery steps.

- Discuss the number of people needed or allowed. One or two people can gather food donations after the farmer's market closes, while it may take dozens to glean a field.

- Determine the type of tools and protection needed. Gleaners may need knives for harvesting from stalks, require skin protection, or need to sign a release form from liability if injured during gleaning.

- Manage facilities. Volunteers may need bathroom facilities, water or food, parking availability or childcare. A volunteer coordinator may be needed for large projects such as gleaning fields or transporting donations from semi-trucks.

- Give detailed instructions. Volunteers need training on safe food handling techniques, harvesting procedures or food recovery protocol.

- Communicate with donors. Farmers, processors, wholesalers and restaurant owners may have specific needs for food recovery. Choose a liaison to speak with donors and problem solve early.

Chapter 44: Community Gardens

In community gardens, urban people share a plot of land to grow plants. Vacated old lots, for example, converted into productive neighborhood gardens beautify the neighborhood and offer a gathering space for all ages. Typically, there is a formal arrangement for supervision and ownership of the land. The municipal government may own or lease the land if they do not manage the garden; nonprofits or cooperatives may also own or manage leased property. A common feature is the active involvement of the gardeners in leasing and managing the space.

Community gardens offer a vibrant food system and familiarize those passing by with local food knowledge. Gardens also offer safe spaces where knowledge and self-reliance pass from one generation to the next. Youth of all ages can be involved in gardening. Gardeners benefit from exercise, inexpensive tasty foods and socialization, while enjoying nature.

In a community garden, you rent one of the divided plots that may be of various sizes. Often, tilling, fencing or watering services are available. Community gardens yield many benefits for gardeners. Participants observe other plots to get ideas about plant spacing, appropriate varieties, weed control, plant support systems and soil amendments. Many share tips about seed saving, companion planting, processing techniques or recipe exchange.

Community gardens are not limited to annual plant production, as there are established gardens decades old with fruit trees or bushes, perennial crops and small egg production areas. A few dedicated spaces have permanent buildings for communal tools, meeting space or certified kitchens. A community garden can become a popular gathering place for neighbors.

Simple Steps to Join a Community Garden

🍎 Contact the American Community Gardening Association (ACGA), a local gardening group or government office such as zoning, parks and recreation or county extension for a community garden location.

🍎 Discuss the garden with the organizers of the space. There may be rules, meetings or assistance.

🍎 If you are a beginning gardener, choose one of the smaller plots so you do not feel overwhelmed with planting, weeding or processing.

🍎 Determine the growing zone that indicates the temperatures in your area. A map of zones is available at www.usna.usda.gov/Hardzone/ushzmap.html. Plant catalogs and seed packets will indicate the zone for the plant.

🍎 Be respectful. In a communal space, cooperative gardening is key. Be sure to keep your plot well tended with regular weeding, walking paths and organized space. If you have small children, restrict access to other plots so as not to damage plants.

🍎 Ask questions. Most fellow gardeners are happy to talk about their experience and share gardening tips. Soon, people will be asking for your advice!

🍎 Enjoy the experience of being in the garden and raising your own food in a community!

Chapter 45:
Food Policy Councils

Consumer action by itself cannot manage the food system as a whole. We must hold decision-makers accountable for wise management and planning for future challenges. Ask your state and national legislator to support farm preservation; promote food production in urban areas; and incorporate local food stipulations into federal funding of schools, food programs and contracts for food services. See the websites below to stay informed.

Food Policy Councils, which are either independent groups or municipal councils, monitor food security, enable communities to produce their own food, and provide healthy food for citizens. These Councils monitor any change that affects food supply or access and also plan for the future. Zoning laws affecting food production, transportation routes to stores, contracts for curb-side compost pick up are examples of food system monitoring by Councils. Find out more about Food Policy Councils at http://www.foodsecurity.org/FPC.

Simple Steps for Local Food Citizens

🍎 Inquire about a Food Policy Council in your area.

🍎 Hold city council and county board members accountable in any decision on local food.

🍎 Regularly check websites that track agriculture, food and nutrition at the national level. These include Food Research and Action Center (www.frac.org), USDA Food and Nutrition Service (www.fns.usda.gov), Farm Aid (www.farmaid.org), Institute for Agriculture and Trade Policy (www.iatp.org) or Food Routes (www.foodroutes.org).

Glossary

Agribusiness: the business of agriculture that can refer to various aspects of food production and the food system. This may also be used negatively when applied to the size of the business and level of influence to the food system.

Biodiversity: the number and variety of organisms, including plants and animals, within a region.

Biodynamic farming: holistic organic farming methods that integrate crops and livestock and manage the bioregion with as few external inputs as possible.

Bioregion: regions defined by natural geographic boundaries and common characteristics rather than political boundaries.

Carbon footprint: effect of your daily decisions on the planet. Gases released contribute to climate change. You can estimate your footprint at www.carbonfootprint.com

Certified Naturally Grown (see Naturally Grown): an alternative certification to the National Organic Program for certification for agricultural practices. See www.naturallygrown.org

Commodities: generally anything that is traded; often inputs used to produce other goods, such as wheat or corn. In this book, commodities refers to the major crops included in the U.S. Farm Bill which includes a list of nonperishable crops, the majority of which were in production in the 1930s.

Community Supported Agriculture (CSA): farms that offer subscriptions or memberships that exchange a flat fee for a designated amount of weekly food produced on the local farm.

Concentrated animal feedlot operations (CAFO): large numbers of animals or poultry confined to a small area without grass or vegetation with waste accumulation that threatens the environment.

Diversified Farm (see also: Monoculture): farms which produce a variety of plants or animals, usually in an integrated system.

EBT: electronic balance transfer cards are used by SNAP/Food Stamp recipients to purchase food.

Eco label: labels which indicate the sustainability of a product.

Ecosystem: a group of living and nonliving things that interact.

Endangered food: foods which are at risk of becoming extinct.

Food and Drug Administration (FDA): a federal agency within the Department of Health and Human Services that regulates all foods except meat and poultry, food additives and dietary supplements.

Factory farm: a farm which has intensive production of animals and birds. See concentrated animal feedlot operation.

Farmers' market: multiple farmers selling food in a central location.

Foodshed: the flow of food, similar to a watershed, from source to elimination; this includes production through processing, distributing, marketing, consuming and ending in disposal.

Food miles: the number of miles that food travels from production to the consumer

Food system: the processes that involve food including producing, processing, distributing, marketing, preparing, consuming and disposing.

Genetically modified organism (GMO): organisms in which the genetic material is altered in a way that does not occur naturally.

Gleaning: clearing a field of food after mechanical harvesting has taken place.

Grass-fed: animals that are fed grass and forage for their lifetime, post weaning.

Herbicide: weedkiller, chemical which kills plants.

Heritage food: foods (fruits, vegetables, animals, birds, etc.) which are at risk of extinction because of lack of production or elimination.

Integrated pest management (IPM): Agricultural system that prevents pest infestation through a variety of preventive controls before applying insecticide.

Insecticide: chemicals that kill insects, often classified as pesticides.

Local food: food produced as close to your home as possible.

Local food movement: efforts across the globe which support a local food system.

Local vs regional (foodshed): contrasts the geographic area where food is available; local is closer to your home, regional is farther away. Regional may be within the next state or multiple states.

Locavore: person who preferentially chooses food grown within 100 miles of their home.

Monoculture (see also: Diversified farm): planting or raising one (mono) crop or animal.

Natural: If labeled, this is defined by the Food and Drug Administration as a product that is minimally processed and does not contain artificial ingredients or added color. For an unlabeled food, this is not defined and may be interpreted in various ways. This is a confusing term since it is not well-defined.

Naturally Grown: may refer to the alternative method of organic production or people may define this for themselves. Unless a farmer is certified, this may not have a clear definition. You will need to ask more questions about production or processing.

Naturally raised meat: livestock raised without growth promoters or antibiotics and never fed animal-byproducts.

Organic: farming which concentrates on soil fertility and does not use chemical fertilizers or pesticides. Certified organic follows the agricultural practices as determined by the National Organics Standards Board of the USDA.

Pastured /Pastured-finished meat: most of the animal's life was spent outdoors on pasture. Variations are possible; ask your farmer what this means.

Pesticide: Substances that prevent, repel or destroy a pest. Pests may include any living organism such as insects, weeds, animals, fungi or bacteria.

Pick Your Own: See "U-Pick"

Plant-based diet: refers to a predominantly plant-, rather than meat-based diet, with variations ranging from an occasional or small proportion of animal products, to entirely plant-based.

Seasonal food: food that is produced during different times of the year. Plants grow during different temperature and moisture conditions.

Slow food: people who celebrate food with local food, heritage crops and food production, and eating in a relaxed atmosphere with family or friends. See www.slowfood.org

Sustainable agriculture: farming that considers current and future agriculture needs and includes environmental health, social equity and economic profitability and parity.

Terrior: the conditions of the geographic area, including climate, soil type, topography, that contribute to the type of food that is grown and the specific tastes from these local conditions.

U-pick (or Pick Your Own): A farm that allows customers to harvest the food directly from the plant.

United States Department of Agriculture (USDA): national department that emphasizes U.S. food, agriculture, and natural resources through many programs. www.usda.gov

Varietals: a biological variety

Resources

Note: To find many more resources than are listed here, including resources specific to each chapter or section, visit the online version. Plus, the links are "clickable," so you don't have to type in website addresses.

http://www.eatlocalsimplesteps.com

General Local Food Resources

County Extension
Throughout this book, "Contact your local extension agent" is often mentioned. Start with these two websites (below) OR search under: "extension agent" or "farm advisor" and "your county & state."
http://www.csrees.usda.gov/Extension
http://www.csrees.usda.gov/qlinks/partners/state_partners.html

Eat Local Challenge
Group blog for folks taking the "eat local" challenge.
http://www.eatlocalchallenge.com

Eat Local Simple Steps
This book's companion website.
http://www.eatlocalsimplesteps.com

Foodroutes Network
Learn more about community based food systems, "Eat local" resources, and "Buy Fresh, Buy Local" campaigns from this non-profit group.
http://foodroutes.org

Locavores
A website from the women who coined the phrase "locavore". Dedicated to eating only foods grown or harvested within a 100 mile radius. Chapters nationwide.
http://www.locavores.com

National Cooperative Grocers Association
Various topics and recipes by coop members and staff.
http://www.eatlocalamerica.coop/eating-local

National Sustainable Agriculture Information Service (ATTRA)
Find out more about local and regional food systems; food and agriculture topics.
https://attra.ncat.org/attra-pub/local_food

Sustainable Table
Educates consumers on local, sustainable food.
http://www.sustainabletable.org

Finding Local Food

Searchable databases by local region (Farmers' markets, CSAs, restaurants featuring local food, farm stands, Pick Your Own, food co-ops, etc.)

ATTRA (National Sustainable Agriculture Information Service)
"Local Food Directories"
Find a local food directory for your region.
https://attra.ncat.org/attra-pub/local_food/search.php

Eat Well Guide
Searchable database for farms, markets, restaurants etc. that feature local food.
www.eatwellguide.org

Field to Plate, "What's in Season"
State by state listings of local foods.
http://www.fieldtoplate.com/guide.php

Local Dirt
Search for farms, businesses, co-ops, farmers' markets and more
https://www.localdirt.com

Local Harvest
Extensive resources to find local, sustainably grown food in your area. Lists farms, farmers' markets, restaurants and more through interactive maps
http://www.localharvest.org

Rodale Institute, Farm Locator
http://www.rodaleinstitute.org/farm_locator

Farmers' Markets

USDA, Agricultural Marketing Service
Searchable database for farmers' markets
http://apps.ams.usda.gov/FarmersMarkets

Community Supported Agriculture (CSA) Farms

Biodynamic Farming and Gardening Association, CSA Resources
http://www.biodynamics.com/csa.html

USDA, Alternative Farming Systems CSA Resource page
http://www.nal.usda.gov/afsic/pubs/csa/csa.shtml

Wilson College, Robyn Van En Center CSA Resources
http://www.wilson.edu/wilson/asp/content.asp?id=804

Co-ops & Natural Food Stores

Cooperative Grocer "Food Coop Directory"
http://www.cooperativegrocer.coop/coops

Newspapers & Magazines

Edible Communities Publications
Home of the "Edible (City)" publications featuring local food.
http://www.ediblecommunities.com

Buying Clubs

Blooming Prairie Natural Foods, "How to Start A Cooperative
Food Buying Club"
http://www.coopdirectory.org/bp003.htm

Local Dirt, "A Cooperative Food-Buying Club Primer"
http://www.localdirt.com/pdf/bc.pdf

Restaurants

Slow Food USA
Local chapters in each state which frequently list restaurants that
use local food.
http://www.slowfoodusa.org

The Chef's Collaborative
Dedicated to educating and encouraging the use of local foods in restaurants.
http://chefscollaborative.org

Pick Your Own (U-Pick)

Pick Your Own
Searchable database, resources, picking tips and more.
http://www.pickyourown.org

Spread the Word (Local Food Movement)

American Farmland Trust
Dedicated to saving farmland and local farms.
http://www.farmland.org

ATTRA's "Local Food Resources," "Policy & Food Access," and more.
https://attra.ncat.org/attra-pub/local_food

Community Food Security Coalition
Categorized list of resources for community food security, sustainable agriculture and food systems, and more.
http://www.foodsecurity.orgError! Hyperlink reference not valid.
FarmAid
Supports family farms with information and resources.
http://www.farmaid.org

National Campaign for Sustainable Agriculture
Dedicated to shaping public policy that promotes a sustainable food and agriculture system.
http://sustainableagriculture.net

National Family Farm Coalition
Focuses on family farms and rural communities.
http://www.nffc.net

USDA, Know your Food, Know Your Farmer
Food and nutrition programs, alternative farming systems and the national organic program, and others.
http://www.usda.gov/wps/portal/usda/knowyourfarmer?navid=K NOWYOURFARMER

Thank you for purchasing Eat Local!
If you or your organization are interested in selling or giving this book to your members or the public, please visit our website for quantity discounts and our reseller program.

www.eatlocalsimplesteps.com
The website takes off where the book ends!

Our vision is to make this book's companion website a helpful, extensive resource for local foods.

- Extensive resource section for each of the chapters in this book with links to other local food websites and resources.
- Ongoing blog by Jasia Steinmetz talking about "local food" latest news and trends and much more.
- Community participation: Guest blogs by leading local food activists and experts.
- Ask the Expert: Ask Jasia questions about local food.
- And much, much more!

More books from New World Publishing!
(Please visit our other website at www.nwpub.net)

Micro Eco-Farming: Prospering from Backyard to Small-Acreage in Partnership with the Earth

Sell What You Sow! The Grower's Guide to Successful Produce Marketing

The New Farmers' Market: Farm-Fresh Ideas for Producers, Managers & Communities

The New Agritourism: Hosting Community and Tourists on Your Farm

New World Publishing: 11543 Quartz Dr. #1, Auburn, CA 95602
(ph) 530-823-3886 • (fx) 815-331-0732
www.eatlocalsimplesteps.com or www.nwpub.net

Jasia Steinmetz

Jasia (Jayne) Steinmetz, author of this book, is a teacher and gardener who believes that good food is vital for good health – and that local, sustainable food is good for not only ourselves but our society. She and her husband, Jeff, live in rural Wisconsin where they grow most of the produce they eat during the year and purchase directly from farmers for the rest of their meals. Jasia's passion is to educate people about the impact of their food choices and to promote a food system that is sustainable for generations. Jasia is a founding member and current Board member of the Central Rivers Farmshed, a community group which promotes local food and supports local farmers. She is also a professor of food and nutrition at the University of Wisconsin and a Registered Dietitian whose teaching career focuses on promoting healthy diets and sustainable, local food systems.

My Eat Local Simple Steps Notes

My Eat Local Simple Steps Notes

My Eat Local Simple Steps Notes

My Eat Local Simple Steps Notes